New Perspectives
on School Integration

Edited by

MURRAY FRIEDMAN   ROGER MELTZER

CHARLES MILLER

D1157817

FORTRESS PRESS   PHILADELPHIA

Acknowledgments

We are grateful to the Samuel S. Fels Fund, its chairman Judge Nochem Winnett, and executive director Dr. Dennis Clark for a grant to hold the conference on which much of this book is based. They are of course not responsible for the contents of this book.

"Teaching Ethnic Studies: Key Issues and Concepts" by James A. Banks is reprinted with the permission of the author from the *Social Studies*, May-June 1975, pp. 107–13.

"Why Johnny Can't—The Problem of State School Financing" by Rochelle L. Stanfield is reprinted with the permission of the *National Journal*, 24 April 1976.

"School Financing Undergoes a Revolution" by Ward Sinclair is reprinted with the permission of the *Washington Post*, 10 July 1978.

"Black Excellence—The Case of Dunbar High School" by Thomas Sowell is reprinted with the permission of the author from the *Public Interest*, no. 35 (Spring 1974), pp. 3–21, © 1974 by National Affairs, Inc.

"Presentation to Massachusetts Legislature—March 30, 1976" by James S. Coleman is reprinted with the permission of the author.

"Urban Desegregation and White Flight: A Response to Coleman" by Thomas F. Pettigrew and Robert L. Green is reprinted with the permission of the authors from *Phi Delta Kappan* (February 1976), vol. 57, pp. 399–402.

"Desegregation and Academic Achievement" by Robert L. Crain and Rita E. Mahard is reprinted with the permission of the authors and Joseph M. Cronin, State Superintendent of Education, State Board of Education, Illinois Office of Education.

Quotations from "Learning Together: A Report on the Regional Cultural Resources Program" are reprinted with the permission of the School District of Philadelphia Board of Education.

Biblical quotations from the Revised Standard Version of the Bible, copyrighted 1946, 1952, © 1971, 1973 by the Division of Christian Education of the National Council of the Churches of Christ in the U.S.A., are used by permission.

Library of Congress Cataloging in Publication Data

Main entry under title:

New perspectives on school integration.

1. School integration—United States—Addresses, essays, lectures.   I.   Friedman, Murray, 1926–
II.   Meltzer, Roger, 1946–   III.   Miller, Charles, 1943–
LC214.2.N48   370.19′342   78-21715
ISBN 0-8006-1359-7

Contents

Those essays marked with an asterisk were given in an earlier form at a symposium held at La Salle College sponsored by the Lutheran Synod of Southeastern Pennsylvania and the Philadelphia Chapter of the American Jewish Committee on June 13, 1978.

iv   Contents

1

School Integration Today: The Case for New Definitions

Murray Friedman

THE YEAR 1979 marked the twenty-fifth anniversary of the Supreme Court decision in *Brown* v. *Board of Education*. The decision of the Court banned not only governmentally required school segregation; it set in motion a civil-rights and, later, race revolution. This opened the door to greater civil rights and opportunities for millions of Americans. It has created profound changes in our thinking as a nation in the quarter of a century that has elapsed since 1954.

It is also true that few issues in public life are more divisive or confounding than school integration.* A number of influential voices to which the community has looked for guidance here have developed reservations both on the goals of and methods used to achieve integration. Most troubling, perhaps, has been public opposition resulting sometimes in violence that has developed in a number of northern cities experiencing school integration, opposition once thought to characterize race relations only in the South.

Curiously enough, all this has taken place against the background of sharp improvement of public attitudes on racial questions and on school desegregation itself. In a study of public attitudes released on August 28, 1978, the Gallup organization reported that the proportion

---

* The word *integration* is used here rather than *desegregation*. Desegregation involves bringing together in the same school or social setting blacks and whites. This may or may not produce integration. The latter means changes in attitudes and associations that go beyond physical commingling on a racial basis to broader acceptance. As used here, also, integration means acceptance across ethnic and religious as well as racial lines. This broadens the issue explored further as will be seen in the body of this chapter.

1

of southern white parents who say they would object to sending their children to a school where half are blacks has declined from 79 in 1963 to 28 percent today. The proportion of white parents living outside the South who would object has declined from 33 to 23 percent.[1]

The confusion that has developed on school desegregation questions in recent years has resulted in contradictory policies. When the Supreme Court, for example, ruled out metropolitan desegregation of the Detroit schools, which were 71 percent black, the NAACP suggested that in order to achieve desegregation each school in that city should have 71 percent black children. Schools varying from this standard by more than 15 percent would be considered segregated. In turning down this plan, the district judge pointed out that under such an arrangement, a school that was 85 percent black would be a desegregated school while one 55 percent black would be considered a segregated white school. Likewise, it has come to be accepted as educationally desirable to assign black teachers to predominantly black schools where they can serve as role models, but a western city that had recruited black teachers especially trained to teach in inner city schools was required not long ago by HEW officials to spread them evenly throughout the system in order to integrate the staff.[2] School desegregation programs have taken some unusual turns in recent years.

Therefore it is appropriate to ask how such a situation has come about. What are the moral and practical implications of this issue today and in the years ahead? Much of the confusion and bitterness we are experiencing stems from the fact that major changes have taken place in American life that have not been fully absorbed into our thinking. To some degree the courts, the community, many civil rights spokesmen, and their critics are frozen into postures formed in 1954 that no longer fit the current situation. In some instances policies and programs which claim to be inspired by *Brown* clearly have led to defeating that decision's objectives. It is for this reason that Professor Derrick Bell, who for a number of years served as counsel for the NAACP and in that capacity directed many cases that sought to make a reality of the *Brown* decision, has referred on one occasion to "the curse of *Brown*." His essay is found in chapter two.

This book is based on a symposium held at La Salle College sponsored by the Lutheran Synod of Southeast Pennsylvania and the Philadelphia Chapter of the American Jewish Committee on June 13, 1978, called "New Perspectives on School Integration." A number of the essays included here and marked with an asterisk were given in an earlier form as papers at this symposium. The others were gathered from specialized journals and other sources and reprinted here because the editors believed they provided the reader with additional new insights on this old problem.

Both the American Jewish Committee and the Lutheran Synod of Southeast Pennsylvania have a long history of active support for and involvement in school integration problems. The essays included in this book are generally in conformity with these beliefs. The authors do not however always agree with the sponsors of the symposium or with one another. On a subject that is so controversial and where there is so much disagreement among specialists in the field, it was felt that opening up a variety of views was the best way to help enlarge our thinking here. There is however a general premise in this volume: *the editors believe that we have reached an impasse on school integration issues that requires a serious reevaluation of where we are going and what we are doing.* We have included a number of essays calculated to show the changes that have taken place in America and the thinking about this subject in the past quarter of a century. Other essays attempt to suggest how schools can take into account these changes and get on with the business of integration and improving equal educational opportunity for all our children.

It is important to note at the outset that while much of the public's attention has been focused on school desegregation controversies, particularly the acrimonious debate and violence growing out of school busing, most of the immediate objectives of the original school desegregation movement launched by *Brown* have been successfully met. That is, the original goal of civil rights forces was the dismantling of school systems segregated under law. Most of these, although not all, were of course in the South. Despite massive resistance that greeted *Brown* and other court decisions, persistent and often courageous efforts on the part of blacks, aided by sympathetic liberal and religious allies, and rulings by the federal courts, forced resistance there to collapse. As a result of compliance agreements and court orders, by 1972 some 46 percent of all southern black students were in schools that were more than 50 percent white. Only 24.5 percent were enrolled in schools that were composed of more than 90 percent minority-group children. In a comparatively short period of time, schools in the South became more desegregated than any other region in the country. This is not to minimize the problems then or now. As the South moved toward greater desegregation, the combination of a hostile Nixon administration—which curtailed desegregation suits entered by the Justice Department—and broader social currents including the movement to the suburbs has often led to resegregation of desegregated schools.[3] The South, in short, has entered the mainstream of American life.

The fact is that in the past quarter of a century there has been a major shift of populations. There was an exodus of blacks out of rural areas in the fifties and sixties into central cities in the North, South, and West, and many middle-class whites, as well as some middle-class blacks, have moved out of these cities into suburban areas. While racial animosities have undoubtedly contributed to this outward flow of whites, other factors are clearly at work here, including the American dream of success and upward mobility, as reflected in a house in the suburbs surrounded by grass and open spaces. The result has been, however, that many of our cities have become increasingly black, and their public-school populations even more so since 1954. Washington, D.C., schools are now 96.5 percent nonwhite, while Atlanta's are 89 percent, Detroit's 83 percent, and San Francisco's 77 percent. From 1968 to 1976, Philadelphia saw a decline of 25 percent in its white school population, a relatively small figure as compared to other cities, but even so, black and Puerto Rican students now comprise some 68 percent of the public-school children. In short, in the past quarter of a century our largest cities have begun to run out of white students with whom to desegregate.

Closely related to this is the fact that a considerable number of the minorities who have come to inherit these cities are poor. In New York alone some 52 percent of its one million public-school students qualify for free lunches; a third of the enrollment is made up of welfare children.[4] With the flight of middle- and upper-middle-class whites and blacks from the cities, the aging of many of these cities, the growth of crime and violence, and decline in city services, the possibilities for school desegregation have been reduced or complicated enormously. It was for this reason that Judge Jack B. Weinstein ruled in the much-discussed Mark Twain Junior High School, Coney

Island, Brooklyn, case in 1974 that the schools should not be held responsible alone for school desegregation. He ruled that city, state, and federal agencies involved in housing, sanitation, police, and other pertinent government services should come together to try to alleviate the conditions that have caused many to withdraw from the area. Judge Weinstein later did not accept the plan of the special master he appointed to accomplish this.

In the late sixties and early seventies, religious and civil-rights leaders thought that the suburbs might provide the missing white school populations with whom blacks could be integrated. It was felt that school desegregation suits would provide metropolitan solutions to the problem of the growing racial isolation in the society. But in *Milliken v. Bradley* in 1974, the Supreme Court refused to endorse such a plan ordered by a lower court in the Detroit area.[5] The majority held that it has not been demonstrated that the suburban districts involved had deliberately participated in creating the situation (state action) and therefore could not be required to provide a solution across school district lines.[6] While some have suggested that the Court's ruling here was not definitive—most recently it has required metropolitan desegregation in Wilmington, Delaware, and its eight surrounding school districts—there is little doubt that the Detroit decision has struck a severe blow against metropolitan desegregation plans.[7]

The *Brown* decision dealt specifically with segregated public schools as a conscious instrument of public policy. More recently the question has emerged, how should we respond to schools that are segregated as a result of the voluntary movement of people rather than through governmental action? Moreover, what responsibility does society have if schools desegregated by law become segregated again as whites decide to move out? It is true that people's choices are not entirely voluntary. Incomes, availability and location of jobs, and other factors prescribe limits. However, this gets into broader social questions that the schools are not equipped to deal with. It is obvious, of course, that public officials have sometimes manipulated school feeder lines and adopted other measures that have contributed to school segregation. In such cases the courts have made it clear that the situation is not different than that *Brown* set out to alleviate. These are instances of de jure segregation (governmentally imposed) that must be struck down, as contrasted with de facto segregation, segregation that arises from private actions. In the latter instance, recent decisions by the Supreme Court in Austin and Dayton seem to suggest there is no government responsibility to rectify the situation.

Here we come to an important aspect of American life that our society has only begun to grapple with seriously in recent years. While the currents flowing in our society that make us look, feel, and think more alike are very strong, many people continue to cling with stubborn tenacity to persons of their own ethnic, racial, and religious background in their neighborhoods or seek to recreate such communities in some form when they move away from them. This is not only a result of outside and discriminatory pressures nor a holdover from a discriminatory past. These patterns are often as strong among middle- and even upper-middle- as well as lower-middle- and working-class elements. The nearness of long-known and culturally similar family, friends, and neighbors, and institutional arrangements such as churches and synagogues give people greater comfort and security. "In a sense, New York is a series of connecting and overlapping villages," Pete Hamill wrote in discussing a recent primary campaign. "There is an Irish village and a black village. There is a Jewish village, an Italian village, a Chinese village, a Polish village and even a WASP village."[8] Italian Americans in Chicago and New York, Rudolph J. Vecoli has suggested recently, "still register a segregation index of well over 50% which means that over half of them would have to move to achieve a random distribution throughout the city."[9] In recent years, an important body of social scientific literature has begun to explore this phenomenon.[10]

The upsurge or, perhaps more accurately, legitimization of ethnic identity since 1954 is a social force of some consequence which has an important relationship to school integration. To some extent it runs counter to or at least simultaneous with pressures that have been in existence throughout American life for assimilation and integration. It has been felt particularly strongly among blacks. When one liberal white organization suggested several years ago to the Urban League in Baltimore that they join together in a suit to require desegregation of the suburbs, the idea was turned down. Now that blacks were developing a political base of power in the city, it was explained, such efforts would dissipate hard-won black power.

While groups like the NAACP and Urban League have continued to press vigorously for school desegregation, other voices, both at the grass-roots level and among a number of black intellectuals, have been heard recently calling for different kinds of approaches to obtaining equal educational opportunity. In the sixties, frustration with the slow pace of desegregation and the desire to improve the quality of education for minority children produced a movement for community control of the schools. More recently, discouraged by the problems of achieving desegregation in Atlanta, which had gone from 32 percent black in 1952 to 82 percent black in 1974, lawyers for the local chapter of the NAACP branch worked out a compromise plan with the Atlanta school board that sought full faculty and employee desegregation but only limited student desegregation. The school board agreed to hire a number of blacks in top-level administrative positions, including a black superintendent of schools. Defending the plan, Dr. Benjamin Mays of that city, one of the most respected black educators in the country, declared:

> We have never argued that the Atlanta Compromise Plan is the best plan, nor have we encouraged any other school system to adopt it. The plan is the most viable plan for Atlanta—a city school system that is 82 percent Black and 18 percent white and is continuing to lose whites each year to five counties that are more than 90 percent white.
>
> . . . More importantly, Black people must not resign themselves to the pessimistic view that a non-integrated school cannot provide Black children with an excellent educational setting. Instead, Black people, while working to implement *Brown*, should recognize that integration alone does not provide a quality education, and that much of the substance of quality education can be provided to Black children in the interim.[11]

When several thousand members of the plaintiffs' class in Atlanta signed a petition favoring the plan, the federal court, apparently influenced by this, approved it. Subsequently, in a move that received national attention, the NAACP ousted the Atlanta branch president who supported it. Similar clashes have developed between grass-roots black opinion and civil-rights leadership in Boston and Detroit as well.[12] The debate over busing that has been going full blast in recent years has taken place seemingly oblivious of the fact that about half of all blacks as well as the great preponderance of whites, as measured by public opinion polls, are opposed to this desegregation device.[13]

With the development of greater black self-assurance in recent years, a number of blacks are questioning the idea that the only way their children can achieve in schools is if they sit next to white children there. Why, many have begun to ask, cannot the educational programs in predominantly black schools be sufficiently improved to accomplish this purpose without disrupting the living patterns of black families? In a critique of a desegregation plan filed by the Boston School Committee in the Boston school case directly to Federal Judge W. Arthur Garrity, almost two dozen black community leaders declared:

> In the name of equity, we . . . seek dramatic improvement in the quality of education available to our children. Any steps to achieve desegregation must be reviewed in light of the black community's interest in improved pupil performance as the primary characteristic of educational equity. We define educational equity as the absence of discriminatory pupil placement and improved performance of all children who have been the objects of discrimination. We think it neither necessary, nor proper to endure the dislocations of desegregation without reasonable assurances that our children will instructionally profit.[14]

As part of this reevaluation underway, UCLA economist Thomas Sowell publicized the experience of the Dunbar High School in Washington, D.C. From 1870 to 1955 this school existed as an elite but segregated black school yet managed to produce an extraordinary collection of leaders, including the first black general (Benjamin O. Davis), the first black federal judge (William H. Hastie), the first black cabinet member (Robert C. Weaver), the discoverer of blood plasma (Charles Drew), and the first black senator since Reconstruction (Edward W. Brooke). One does not have to support segregated schools or share Sowell's political philosophy to recognize the validity of his point: that black schools don't have to be automatically bad and in fact can be quite good. (See chapter nine.)[15] Moreover, elite black schools are not the only ones that have had success in motivating and educating black children. The late Marcus Foster won national attention and promotion to superintendent of the Oakland (California) Public Schools (where he was murdered by Symbionese Liberation Army zealots) for his success as principal of Gratz High School, located in a socially disadvantaged and virtually all-black neighborhood in Philadelphia. More recently, black parents in the predominantly black Providence–St. Mel's parochial high school in Chicago publicly challenged the decision of the diocese when in an economy move it decided to close the school; the parents argued that their children were receiving a superior education there.

The *Brown* decision made it unconstitutional to assign children to public schools on the basis of race. This is not the same thing, however, as requiring all schools to be desegregated. Twenty-five years after *Brown*, it seems necessary to point out that every predominantly black school is not necessarily a segregated school. If this were the case, every school in a predominantly Italian, Jewish, or some other ethnic neighborhood—to say nothing of every school in Africa— would have to be considered segregated.

The growing emphasis on racial and ethnic diversity in American life in recent years has been augmented, further, by changes in our immigration laws which affect this question. Under the Johnson Act passed and signed into law in 1965, the racist "national origins" quota system was abandoned. As a result, increasing numbers of people have been arriving in this country from the Far East, eastern and southern Europe, and the western hemisphere. The influx of Hispanics added to Spanish-speaking groups already here has reached a point where in 1975 the Census Bureau estimated there are now 11.2 million living in this country.[16] The post-1965 wave of new immigrants is the largest since the period of mass immigration to this country in the 1880s accounting for a third of the population increase in the United States today. Nor do these figures take into consideration the approximately eight million illegal aliens the U.S. Immigration and Naturalization Service estimates now live here.[17]

As a result of these population changes, many of our cities are coming to take on the character of these new or newly emerging immigrant streams and rising ethnic forces. Mostly Polish, Hamtramck in Michigan has been renewed by Yugoslavians and Albanians who play cards and drink thick Turkish coffee in coffeehouses that act as community centers.[18] Cuban culture has made Tampa, Florida, into a virtually Cuban city. In New York, one can read a Haitian newspaper, dine in a Cuban restaurant, dance to a Dominican merengue, play "Kumkim" and "Aces Wild," Greek card games, in a Democratic club, and vote, increasingly, for Puerto Rican candidates for office. In Los Angeles, Mexican Americans have overtaken and now surpass in size the black population.

The schools have had to adjust to these important changes. Faced with a heavy influx of Cuban refugees, Dade County (Miami),

Florida, set up in 1963 the first bilingual education program in the country since World War I. Civil rights activism in the sixties produced, also, a number of lawsuits aimed at improving the education of non-English-speaking students. This resulted in the passage of the Bilingual Education Act in 1968 and brought about the first federal funding for such education. In a landmark ruling in a suit brought on behalf of Chinese students in San Francisco in 1974, the Supreme Court held that children with a limited grasp of English were deprived of equal treatment if schools made no effort to address their linguistic problems. This was held to be a violation of Title VI of the 1964 Civil Rights Act. In the decade since the act was passed, the number of bilingual programs in the United States has grown from seventy-two to more than five hundred, with a corresponding leap in federal appropriations from $7 million to $150 million.[19]

Many civil rights leaders have been pressing for school desegregation programs including the use of busing. It is easy to understand and sympathize with efforts to rectify the injustices of the past and present. Is it fair, however, to prevent Chinese American children from attending schools convenient to the afternoon neighborhood private schools they also attend, as a federal judge did several years ago when he ordered them to be bused as part of a San Francisco desegregation plan? Similarly, is it "equal protection of the law" in the same case to keep Spanish-speaking children from attending schools in which their numerical dominance has brought about bilingual classes and specially trained teachers?[20] In the fall of 1977, the Office of Civil Rights declared several bilingual classrooms in New York City to be segregated. What about Jewish and Roman Catholic children who find it difficult to attend after-school religious classes as a result of the lengthened day resulting from school busing programs? These are new questions that have arisen since the Supreme Court's 1954 ruling.

The "rise of the unmeltable white ethnics" (to use Michael Novak's phrase) has added still another dimension to the problem. Much like the civil-rights and race revolution which brought about the growth of black studies programs, the renewed interest in group identity has had a similar effect. In 1972, Congress passed and the president signed into law the Ethnic Heritage Studies Program.[21] Its purpose, as stated in the act, is "to afford students opportunities to know more about the nature of their own heritage and to study the cultural heritage of other ethnic groups in the nation." This has spurred a movement to incorporate into social studies and other curricula materials used in the schools knowledge about the history and experiences of Italians, Poles, Jews, Irish, and other ethnic groups as well as blacks. In chapter five Professor James Banks, one of the leaders of this movement, discusses the rationale for as well as the specifics of such programs.[22]

In the light of the continued importance of religious and ethnic diversity in American life, it becomes necessary also to take a closer look at the nation's private and parochial schools. A large proportion of the students attending nonpublic schools in our big cities today are going to Roman Catholic schools. The rest go to Lutheran, Jewish, or nonsectarian schools. In Philadelphia, archdiocesan schools account for about 40 percent of the city's total school population. While Catholic schools have recently passed through a period of great difficulty resulting from inflation and declining vocations of priests and nuns, forcing a greater reliance on lay teachers, the situation appears to have stabilized. These schools are an important part of the total American education system.

There has been a sharp increase in recent years in the number of black, mainly Protestant children attending these schools. Since 1970, according to Thomas Vitullo-Martin, the figure has doubled. It is now estimated to be 8 percent. In our largest cities, he indicates, blacks comprise between 12 and 60 percent of Catholic-school populations.[23] Black parents believe the education in these schools is better. They like also the greater discipline that is found there in contrast with some slum schools. Efforts to achieve greater integration cannot ignore these schools. (See chapter six by Vitullo-Martin on the role of private schools.) Gary Orfield has suggested that we should consider federal grants to parochial schools for carrying out desegregation plans, but this might be precluded by the First Amendment.[24] At the very least there is a need for greater cooperation between them and the public schools consistent with the First·Amendment, such as in shared time or dual enrollment programs. The Regional Resources Program of the Philadelphia schools described in chapter fifteen provides an example of how this might be done.

One of the reasons the school integration movement became such an important public issue was the belief that this was a means of improving the deplorable education received by many minority-group children. In recent years this effort has turned increasingly to the arena of fiscal equity. The spark was lit in 1967 when the principal of an elementary school in East Los Angeles called in John Anthony Serrano, a Mexican American, and told him that the school, located in a poor Chicano neighborhood, could not provide his children with a good education. Serrano filed suit the following year on behalf of himself and other dissatisfied parents. He charged that the state of California was providing substantially inferior educational opportunities to many children, particularly black, Spanish-surnamed, and other minority-group children, since the money derived from local property or real-estate taxes to support the schools in slum neighborhoods was less than in wealthier areas.[25]

The California Supreme Court ruled in favor of Serrano in 1971. Later, in a case widely seen as establishing the precedent in school financing—*San Antonio Independent School District* v. *Rodriguez*—the U.S. Supreme Court ruled that while education is not a federal right guaranteed by the Fourteenth Amendment, local lawmakers can effect fiscal reform. Since *Serrano* and *Rodriguez*, legal challenges to the system of financing education around the country have accelerated dramatically. By 1978, five states had ruled that state legislatures have an obligation to devise better and more egalitarian ways of financing school districts, and litigation is pending in at least fifteen other states. As a result, billions of additional dollars have been poured into or authorized for poorer school districts by state legislatures in Texas, California, Washington, and Connecticut.[26]

As with most efforts to reform the schools, particularly in their work with minority-group youngsters, the fiscal equity approach appears to have been less successful than its proponents had hoped. The reasons for this go beyond the parameters of this essay. One of the most important, however, is that schools in large urban centers suffer from a tangle of pathologies that require not equal but substantially more funding than their more affluent neighbors. Some states, including Illinois and Minnesota, have made additional state aid available to districts where the concentration of hard-to-educate pupils exceeds the state average.[27]

In this respect, a decision of the New York State Supreme Court on June 23, 1978, has raised hopes that the tax equity approach may still provide an important advance in equal educational opportunity. In *Levittown* v. *Nyquist*, the court upheld the contention of Levittown (joined by the four largest cities in the state) that the proportions of disadvantaged children in their communities created "educational overburden" and limited their ability to provide equal educational opportunities. It ruled that "something more than average aid to school districts must be furnished to accomplish this goal." It seems reasonable to hope, therefore, that minority children in the cities and other disadvantaged areas will end up better off since long-obscured inequities have been highlighted and the requirement for greater funding accepted. However, the taxpayers' revolt, as represented by the Proposition 13 movement, may act as a countervailing force. The fiscal equity movement is discussed in chapters seven and eight by Rochelle Stanfield and Ward Sinclair.[28]

Perhaps the most perplexing of the many changes that have occurred since 1954 has been in how social scientists have come to view the effects of desegregation, particularly the means employed in bringing it about. When the Supreme Court ruled unanimously in *Brown* and the other school cases in 1954 that segregated schools were unlawful, it based its decision not only on the "equal protection of the law" clause of the Fourteenth Amendment. It went on to point out that "modern authority" demonstrated that "To separate [children] from others of similar age and qualifications solely because of their race generates a feeling of inferiority as to their status in the community that may affect their hearts and minds in a way unlikely ever to be undone."[29] In support of this the Court cited seven social science documents in its famous footnote 11. Rather than resting its decision alone on the law and its interpretation by the courts, in short, the High Court invoked social scientific authority.

In the first flush of the civil rights revolution, this caused no special problems. There was fairly wide consensus among social scientists both as to the pernicious effects of racial discrimination and the role of segregated schools in promoting this. As late as 1966, the highly publicized study commissioned by Congress *Equality of Educational Opportunity*, more popularly known as "the Coleman Report," prepared under the direction of Professor James S. Coleman of the University of Chicago, found "that children from disadvantaged backgrounds did somewhat better in schools that were predominantly middle class than in schools that were homogeneously lower class." This was widely taken to mean that educational progress for minority children was improved by school desegregation.[30] Coleman later testified in a Washington, D.C., school desegregation case brought by Julius Hobson and was cited by U.S. Judge J. Skelly Wright to support the court's finding that "Negro students' educational achievement improved when they transfer into white or integrated educational institutions."

More recently, however, acrimonious debate has broken out among social scientists mainly over the techniques for achieving desegregation and their effects. In a widely reported article in the summer of 1972 David Armor, then at Harvard, basing his theories on five local studies, argued that court-ordered, or as more commonly described, "forced," busing did not improve the education of black children, as measured by standardized tests or the relations between black and white children brought together in this way.[31]

Even more dramatically, Coleman in a series of interviews, articles in popular magazines, affidavits in the Boston school desegregation case, an address before a national conference on alternatives to busing, and in a study using data from the Office of Civil Rights of HEW (along with Sara Kelly and John Moore) seemed to be in retreat from his former position. In the large cities, and to a lesser extent in the medium-sized cities, particularly if it involves the busing of whites to black schools, he wrote, "desegregation does produce a loss of whites in the year of desegregation. The loss is intensified in both sets of cities when the city district is surrounded by predominantly white suburban districts in the same metropolitan area." More recently he was quoted as saying that desegregation had provided few academic opportunities for minority students.

The conclusions of Armor, Coleman, and others have been sharply challenged. Thomas F. Pettigrew and Robert L. Green fired back in the February 1976 issue of the Harvard Educational Review. They charged that Coleman's research was methodologically and conceptually faulty and provided no basis for his highly publicized conclusion that urban school desegregation led to "white flight." They criticized him as having been selective in his choice of school districts and for failing to distinguish between his scientific findings and his personal beliefs. Their own analysis of districts with more than seventy-five thousand pupils revealed no correlation between the degree of desegregation and the rate of "white flight."[32]

As the debate over "white flight" has proceeded, however, it has narrowed somewhat. Boston University political scientist Christine

Rossell, who had sharply criticized Coleman's white flight thesis in an article in the *Political Science Quarterly* (Winter 1975–76), has acknowledged more recently that the "major argument" of the Coleman-Kelly-Moore study "has been substantiated empirically." She concedes "an implementation year effect" from court-ordered desegregation that can produce "white flight" initially but sees "no long-term decline since the effect is only short term."[33] In response to Coleman's recent remarks on achievement, twenty-four scholars on a Duke University panel argued that a number of studies showed significant black gains under certain circumstances.[34] Nevertheless the debate over "white flight," achievement, and improved race relations in the schools as a result of desegregation goes on. In chapters ten, eleven, and twelve we have included articles by Coleman, Pettigrew and Green, Robert L. Crain and Rita E. Mahard to give the reader some sense of the confusion that exists when one looks to "modern authority" for guidance here.

What are we to make of the changes in the social and psychological climate that have taken place since 1954? Clearly, proponents of school desegregation have been thrown on the defensive. In terms of public attitudes, the thinking of a significant group of specialists, and to some degree even the courts, there has been some movement away from what is popularly described as "forced" desegregation and racial balancing techniques, especially in de facto segregation situations, even though a number of school systems, including Los Angeles and Wilmington, began court-ordered school busing programs after long delays in the fall of 1978. The focus for many seems to be shifting to attempts to improve the quality of the education in the schools wherever children happen to be, so long as there was and is no official policy and practice of segregation. "The first priority of the schools must be to concentrate on basic skills in the elementary years," Diane Ravitch writes.[35] "Children who enter junior high school without knowing how to read, write, or compute already have two strikes against them. Rarely do the junior and senior high schools have the staff to bring them up to grade level, and these students tend to become truants or discipline problems." Ravitch goes on to suggest that "schools must have the resources needed to deliver quality education. Children from poor homes need individual assistance and a consistent, supportive environment."[36] In his essay in the book (see chapter two), Professor Bell says that we must seek to identify public schools "serving poor, non-white children . . . in an educationally effective fashion." The ingredients of such effective schools, he suggests, include effective leadership, close parental involvement in the educational process, and accountable teachers. "What courts need now are 'equal opportunity' plans containing these components."

While one recognizes the importance of such qualitative improvements, it is nevertheless disturbing to see the growing racial isolation in our schools. We have relearned—to our advantage—the importance of group identity. But this in no way obviates the importance of ethnic outsiders joining the mainstream of American life. The social horizons of minority-group children, particularly if they grow up in economically depressed circumstances, are probably circumscribed in some degree, even when more effective educational programs in isolated schools are developed. Moreover, it is too easy for the community's attention to be withdrawn from such schools, resulting in a failure to provide the resources and extra resources necessary to improve the quality of education there. We know also from Alice Miel's study *The Shortchanged Children of Suburbia*, and common observation, that children who grow up in presumably more favored circumstances without experience with racially and economically different children may form an image of them that is conducive to the development and maintenance of racial myths. While the social costs for court-ordered or mandatory busing may on the whole be too high to pay, as Nancy St. John and others seem to argue, Homer Floyd, the experienced executive director of the Pennsylvania Human Relations Commission, suggests in chapter three that in smaller or moderate-size cities, even "forced" busing can work. That is, he argues, minority-group children appear to do better and there is no diminishment in the educational accomplishments of the majority school population. From this he concludes that it could work in big cities were it not for resistance condoned by public authorities.

All in all, however, the intervening years since *Brown* have shown us that we have tended to look at school desegregation too mechanistically. It is necessary to examine more closely *the kind* of desegregation that takes place. Desegregation is not a unitary thing. As Nancy St. John has shown in her book *School Desegregation: Outcomes For Children*, if it is undertaken under the wrong circumstances, little good and much harm can be engendered.[37] In schools where teachers report little racial tension, for example, black children seem to achieve more, and more positive racial attitudes ensue than in tense, merely desegregated schools.[38] The individual characteristics of children must be taken, also, into consideration. "Desegregation is noticeably more likely to have a positive impact on black test scores," Crain and Mahard report, "if it begins in the earliest grades, and effects are especially likely to be positive for first graders"[39] (see chapter twelve). Younger children, black males, the black middle class, and high achievers apparently benefit more from desegregation. At times, however, it may be desirable for a school in a heavily populated black area that might be working well, as in the case of Marcus Foster's Gratz High School in Philadelphia or the pre-1954 Dunbar School in Washington, D.C., to avoid being dismantled on the grounds of some purely numerical standard of physical desegregation.

The results of twenty-five years of experience with school desegregation or integration in large cities, the community reaction, and the demographic changes that have occurred in this time seem to suggest that policymakers would do well, particularly in de facto segregation situations, to try to develop those programs aimed at maximizing desegregation and equal educational opportunity that can win support from both the majority and minority-group populations rather than seek arbitrary white-black numerical ratios or racial balance opposed by most whites and many blacks. Whatever may have been the need in the late fifties and early sixties to undergo the social disruption in order to dismantle de jure segregation, at this point in time and with virtually all such segregation ended, pressures upon the population to arrange themselves in some kind of racial mix foreign to their lives worked out by outsiders seem likely to be dysfunctional. We do not know all the factors in people's movements, but when voters in Cleveland turned down, recently, a school tax increase as a means of expressing their anger at school busing, Boston's enrollment declined from ninety-eight to seventy-three thousand following a federal court order to desegregate the schools in 1974, and Los Angeles white pupils went from 219,300 to 165,361 in the two years prior to court-ordered busing in the fall of 1978, it seems clear that neither the goal of integration nor improving the quality of education is being accomplished. The fact that violence does not ensue following initiation of a court-ordered school busing program does not make that program necessarily a success.[40]

In this book we have included several essays describing voluntary desegregation programs. In chapter fourteen Horace Seldon describes METCO, a voluntary desegregation program in which some three thousand black children in Boston are bused to several nearby and predominantly white suburban school districts in a program worked out between mostly black parents and these school systems. Such programs can be facilitated, Coleman has suggested, by financial incentives, as is done in Wisconsin, both to sending and receiving schools.[41]

Gary Orfield has backed the "metropolitan open enrollment" plan of Representative Richardson Preyer of North Carolina, which would allow minority students to transfer to suburban systems with federal funds paying the cost.[42] Philadelphia's experimental regional resources program, now no longer in existence because of lack of funds, was built around the idea of taking elementary-grade students from predominantly white and black public and parochial schools for half a day once a week to the famed Franklin Institute. Parents had no difficulty accepting this since their children were receiving an enriched science program. (At one point, when white mothers were putting their children on buses taking them to the Franklin Institute, a number of their neighbors were gathered at the school administration building in a noisy demonstration protest of a school desegregation program that included busing.) In chapter thirteen John Vannoni describes his experience as principal of the new Philadelphia High School of Performing Arts which was created under joint city and federal funding as a magnet school experiment in desegregation. This is particularly impressive. When a situation is created where a school is 53 percent white and 47 percent black and there is a waiting list of one thousand to get in, you must be doing something right.

In all these cases, the parents and children involved were given a chance to choose whether or not to participate. In addition, parents had fairly good reason to believe that their children were going to receive a special or better educational experience that they could not receive in their neighborhood school while at the same time being exposed to children of other racial backgrounds. If there is anything the past twenty-five years has shown beyond any doubt, the central issue for white and black parents alike is not desegregation but how to obtain a better education for their children. The Philadelphia High School of Performing Arts' successful experience with desegregation provides us with still another insight. In recent years "magnet schools" have been advanced as a special device for increasing desegregation. Yet the evidence suggests that most have not been particularly successful in accomplishing this.[43] To do so, it would appear, a "magnet school" must represent a change in the total atmosphere. It is not particularly useful to create a new program, place it in a segregated and failure-prone environment and call it a "magnet school." The Philadelphia High School of Performing Arts was created de novo in the Philadelphia College of Art in the commercial center of the city, and students from all sections were invited to apply for admission.

To be sure, the school experiences cited here can quite properly be described as only "a drop in the bucket" in overcoming racial isolation. Even if they were widely expanded, as we would hope, they can only touch a small proportion of de facto segregation that now exists in the schools. The only response that can be given to this is that the problem is made no better by existing school desegregation strategies which sometimes exacerbate the situation. It is for this reason that it may be necessary to develop new definitions of integration that include but go beyond exact numerical ratios, quotas, or racial balance.

In chapter four, urbanologist Irving Levine lays out such an approach in his concept of a "pluralistic education index" to be used in measuring a school system's program here. This calls not only for rearrangement by the school system of feeder lines of nearby schools and other devices such as integrating teachers to encourage physical desegregation (to the degree this is possible, given the demographic realities in many of our cities today); it also asks whether the system has made arrangements for students to voluntarily go out of their neighborhoods to schools in other sections of the city or suburbs, used alternative schools or arrangements like Philadelphia's High School of Performing Arts, held schools serving predominantly minority-group children to strict forms of accountability, encouraged close parental involvement, developed multicultural and bilingual educational programs, been the recipient of equal or additional funding by the city or state for schools with special urban disabilities and other measures. When a school system has been found to have undertaken a significant number of such activities under this index, he suggests that civil rights groups, the courts, and the public generally consider it to be engaged in appropriate integration and equal educational opportunity programming. It is interesting to note that in the second Detroit decision following the rebuff received by civil rights groups pressing for metropolitan desegregation, the Supreme Court appears to have focused on the quality of education of children in black schools rather than on physical desegregation alone.[44]

It may be that some will look upon the approaches discussed here as a retreat. The "pluralistic education index" developed by Levine— in the main, voluntary forms of integration—we believe provides (1) a realistic approach to the type of desegregation and integration possible today and (2) a means of measuring progress. We wish to make it clear that in spite of the many changes that have taken place in American life in the last twenty-five years, we believe a school system and a society that is more desegregated is, in the main, healthier than one that is not. We need, therefore, the reminder with which Ruth Wick closes this book that desegregation continues to remain a valid and desirable goal. The real issue is how to accomplish this and equal educational opportunity more broadly in the light of changing circumstances. It is our hope that this book will contribute in some small measure to broadening understanding of this problem.

NOTES

1. George Gallup, "Poll Shows Dramatic Drop in U.S. Bias," *San Francisco Chronicle*, 28 September 1978.

2. Diane Ravitch, "Integration, Segregation, Pluralism," *American Scholar*, Spring 1976, pp. 212–13.

3. Elliot Zashin, "The Progress of Black Americans in Civil Rights: The Past Two Decades Assessed," *Daedalus*, Winter 1978, p. 243.

4. B. R. Gifford et al., *School Profiles, 1975–77* (New York: New York City Board of Education, 1977), p. 19.

5. *Milliken v. Bradley*, 418 U.S. 717 (1974).

6. Zashin, "The Progress of Black Americans," p. 244; Derrick A. Bell, Jr., "Serving Two Masters: Integration Ideals and Client Interests in School Desegregation Litigation," *Yale Law Journal* 85, no. 4 (March 1976): 484.

7. The central issue here is whether a governmental unit has practiced or there has been state action that required or facilitated racial segregation. In Wilmington, and Delaware generally, this had occurred, hence the Court order to desegregate across school district lines. As recently as September 1, 1978, U.S. Supreme Court Justice William J. Brennan refused to block court-ordered busing to accomplish metropolitan desegregation (*Philadelphia Inquirer*, 2 September 1978).

8. *Philadelphia Inquirer*, 17 September 1977.

9. Rudolph J. Vecoli, "The Coming of Age of the Italian Americans: 1945–1964," *Ethnicity* 5, no. 2 (June 1978): 124.

10. See Caroline Golab, *Immigrant Destinations* (Philadelphia: Temple University Press, 1977). In his study of residential segregation among white, European-born foreign stock (first- and second-generation Americans) in 1960, Nathan Kantrowitz reported that despite growing homogenization in American life foreign-stock Norwegians tended to live apart from Swedes, Irish from Italians. The physical separation between Norwegians and Russians (mostly Jews) and Russians and blacks was even higher. Kantrowitz predicted that 1970 census materials if studied carefully would make little change. *Ethnic and Racial Segregation in the New York Metropolis: Residential Patterns Among White Ethnic Groups, Blacks and Puerto Ricans* (New York: Praeger Publishers, 1973).

11. Mays's comment: "Atlanta—Living with Brown Twenty Years Later," *Black Law Journal* 3 (1974): 184, 190, 191–92, as quoted by Bell, "Serving Two Masters," pp. 486–87.

12. Bell, "Serving Two Masters," pp. 470, 480–84.

13. See Mary A. Golladay and Jay Noell, *The Condition of Education*, Fourth Annual Report of the National Center for Education Statistics (Washington, D.C.: Government Printing Office, 1978).

14. As quoted by Bell, "Serving Two Masters," p. 470.

15. See also Sowell's more recent comments, "Are Quotas Good for Blacks?" *Commentary*, June 1978, p. 43.

16. The major subgroups are: Mexican origin (6.7 million), Puerto Rican (1.7 million), and Cuban (743 thousand). See *El Tiempo Bicentario* no. 3, 1976.

17. "Now a Growing Source of Immigrants From Asia," *U.S. News and World Report*, 26 November 1973, p. 30; Michael Piore, "The Illegals," *New Republic*, 22 February 1975, pp. 7–8; *Pittsburgh Post Gazette*, 9 December 1976.

18. *New York Times*, 6 January 1974.

19. *Philadelphia Inquirer*, 4 June 1978.

20. Nathan Glazer, "Is Busing Necessary?" *Commentary*, March 1972, p. 45.

21. Title IX of the Elementary and Secondary Education Act.

22. See also Judith Herman, *The Schools and Group Identity* (New York: Institute on Pluralism and Group Identity, 1974); James A. Banks, ed., *Curriculum Guidelines for Multiethnic Education*, Position Statement (Washington, D.C.: National Council for the Social Studies, 1976).

23. Thomas Vitullo-Martin, "Inner-City Option: Catholic Schools," *New York Times*, 14 November 1976.

24. Gary Orfield, *Must We Bus?* (Washington, D.C.: 1978), Brookings Institution, p. 452.

25. In a friend-of-the-court brief filed with the California Supreme Court subsequently, experts gave as an example of the "bizarre maldistribution of resources" Beverly Hills with $50,885 behind each student on which taxes could be leveled and Baldwin Park with only $3,697. The former school district spent $1,232 per student and the latter $577 even though Baldwin Park's tax rate was more than twice that of its neighbor.

26. *New York Times*, 25 June 1978.

27. *New York Times*, 16 July 1978.

28. Phyllis Myers, "Second Thoughts on the Serrano Case," *City*,

Winter 1971, pp. 38–41; "Big Win for Large-City School Districts," *New York Times*, 16 July 1978.

29. *Brown* v. *Board of Education*, 347 U.S. 483 (1954).

30. *New York Times Magazine*, 24 August 1975, p. 10; "Integration Benefits Discounted" (interview with James S. Coleman), *Washington Post*, 18 September 1978.

31. David Armor, "The Evidence on Busing," *Public Interest*, Summer 1972, pp. 90–126.

32. Thomas F. Pettigrew and Robert L. Green, "School Desegregation in Large Cities: A Critique of the Coleman 'White Flight' Thesis," *Harvard Educational Review* 46, no. 1 (1976): 1–53.

33. *New York Times*, 11 June 1978; Christine Rossell, "A Response to 'The White Flight' Controversy," *Public Interest*, Fall 1978, pp. 109–11.

34. *New York Times*, 26 November 1978.

35. See Diane Ravitch's critique of Rossell, "The White Flight Controversy," *American Scholar*, Spring 1978, pp. 135–49, and their exchange in *Public Interest*, Fall 1978. This issue contains a brief summary, also, by David Armor of his recent study "White Flight, Demographic Transition, and the Future of School Desegregation," Rand Corporation, August 1978.

36. *Philadelphia Inquirer*, 19 December 1977.

37. Nancy St. John, *School Desegregation: Outcomes for Children* (New York: John Wiley & Sons, 1975).

38. *Racial Isolation in the Public Schools* (Washington, D.C.: Government Printing Office, 1967), pp. 157–58.

39. Robert L. Crain and Rita E. Mahard, *Desegregation and Black Achievement*, National Review Panel on School Desegregation Research (Durham, N.C.: Institute of Policy Sciences and Public Affairs, Duke University).

40. *New York Times*, 16 April 1978, 19 July 1978, and 7 November 1978.

41. Coleman, "Incentives Schemes for School Desegregation," unpublished paper prepared for the American Academy Study Group on Urban Desegregation, May 1978.

42. Orfield, *Must We Bus?* p. 442.

43. See Stephen Franklin, "Magnet Schools Fail in Philadelphia," *Integrated Education* issue 90 (November–December 1977), vol. 15, no. 6, pp. 95–96; Myrna Oliver, "20 of 46 Magnet Schools Fail To Meet Ethnic Balance," *Los Angeles Times*, 10 August 1978.

44. See Irving M. Levine's essay in chapter four.

2
Defining Brown's Integration Remedy for Urban School Systems

Derrick A. Bell, Jr.

WHITE PARENTS IN a western city recently went to court seeking an order requiring a school system to transfer their son from one high school to another. The judge hearing the case learned that the parents wanted their son reassigned to a high school whose enrollment was 95 percent white. The boy had been assigned initially to a school with a 65 percent black and 35 percent white student population. The school board, in denying the transfer request, relied on Supreme Court precedents dating back to 1963 which bar students from making "minority to majority" transfers in school systems undergoing desegregation.[1] That is, white students can't transfer from schools where whites are in the minority to other schools where whites are in the majority, and vice versa.

But notwithstanding these decisions, the lawyer for the white student argued strenuously that the requested transfer would place his client in a more "racially balanced" school. The lawyer was stopped in his tracks when the judge asked him how a 95 percent white school could be considered more integrated than a 35 percent white school?

The lawyer's inability to answer this mathematically obvious question provides an almost classic insight into how our society has come to define an integrated school as one with a predominantly white student body, with perhaps 5 to 10 percent black or other nonwhite students. This definition prevails, even though its realization has become virtually impossible to attain within urban school districts in this country, most of which are predominantly nonwhite.

23

The belief, obviously deeply held, was that a school with a 95 percent white pupil-population was—for that reason—better integrated than a school with only a 35 percent white pupil-population. For them integration, particularly in the public school context, means that whites will dominate in both numbers and in matters of policy control. A predominantly black school, on the other hand, even one with a substantial white minority (i.e., 35 percent) is, for that reason, suspect, "not integrated," and to be avoided at all costs. To the extent that similar views are held and acted upon by other white parents, the school soon becomes, in fact as well as in white perception, a mainly black school.

But whites are not alone in this tendency to equate integrated schools with predominantly white schools and to view only the latter as effective, legitimate educational institutions. The only black school board member of one of the nation's largest urban school systems asked recently, "But of what value is it to teach black children to read and write in all-black schools?"

The question boggles the mind in its unthinking acceptance of a definition that "whiteness" is an essential ingredient to effective schooling for blacks. The assumption that even the attaining of academic skills is worthless unless those skills are acquired in the presence of white students illustrates dramatically how a legal precedent, namely the Supreme Court's decision in Brown v. Board of Education,[2] has been so constricted even by advocates that its goal—equal educational opportunity—is rendered inaccessible, even unwanted, unless it can be obtained through racial balancing of the school population. Both the philosophy expressed in the black school board member's question and the willingness of white parents to invest good money pursuing in the courts a mathematical absurdity reflect the misconceived views of school integration held by a large percentage of the population.

One might ask how so many people, black and white, arrived at a conclusion that predominantly black schools are, by definition, so inherently deficient that any educational skills acquired in them are rendered valueless. Certainly nothing in the Brown decision requires such a conclusion. Perhaps more importantly, unless this generally held but clearly erroneous view is altered, there is little or no hope that urban school systems will soon provide the equal educational opportunity promised in Brown more than two decades ago.

The "true believer" fervor of traditional school desegregation proponents is reflected in their unwillingness or inability to face what to
them must be depressing demographic, racial facts in our urban areas.
Recent statistics indicate that approximately one-half of the country's
minority children reside in the twenty to thirty largest school districts.
These districts average 60 percent nonwhite, and of the twenty-nine
largest districts only eight still have a white majority.[3] The percentages of minority students in the nation's ten largest districts are
worth reciting. They are: New York City, 69.5 percent; Los Angeles,
63 percent; Chicago, 75 percent; Houston, 65.8 percent; Detroit,
81.3 percent; Philadelphia, 68.2 percent; Miami, 59 percent; Baltimore, 75.6 percent; Dallas, 61.9 percent; and Cleveland, 62.9 percent.[4]

We know from past experience that any effort to implement a
system-wide desegregation order depending on racial balance will require a tremendous amount of busing. The busing orders will be
followed by massive white flight, as has occurred in such cities as
Boston and San Francisco. I concede that there is a great deal of controversy as to whether school desegregation orders spark white flight,
or whether middle-class whites (and blacks as well) leave the urban
schools because of a continuing trend toward the suburbs.[5] But in the
aftermath of city school desegregation orders relying on racial balance
remedies, the percentage of nonwhite students usually increases.
Moreover, those whites and blacks left in the system tend to be from
the lower socioeconomic classes. Even the most idealistic of integration proponents would not urge that these groups are likely to gain
much in racial understanding from attending the same schools.

Moreover, when blacks are integrated into poor white schools, the
long-assumed tactical advantage of *Brown*—"that black kids will get
what white kids get only when black kids are placed in schools where
white kids are"—breaks down. In all too many instances, schools serving poor white children are no better and sometimes worse than
schools serving poor black children. The hostility of the poor whites,
as the Boston experience illustrates all too well, renders any education
at all next to impossible for a long period.

A difficult, even violent transitional period might be worth the
effort and the risk if experience indicated that at some point the
desegregated school settled down and minority students began achieving scholastically at an impressive rate. Again, the studies in this area
evoke more controversy than consensus, but the definitive if provoca-

tive review of those studies by Nancy St. John[6] requires the conclusion that many minority students attending desegregated schools have not experienced educational gain. As another school expert, Ron Edmonds of the Harvard Graduate School of Education, puts it, desegregation helps some black students, harms others, and leaves most of them about the same as far as scholastic performance is concerned.[7] Since the great hope of school desegregation was that black children would close the academic achievement gap between themselves and white children, a policy that is expensive, time-consuming, and disruptive should promise more than simply leaving black students no better off than they were in uniracial schools.

Government civil rights agencies and nationally recognized civil rights groups have treated the just-summarized obstacles to full school desegregation as no different than the resistance which they have overcome by courageous persistence during the last two decades. In litigation, they have continued to press for desegregation plans that maximize racial balance throughout the system. Despite the barriers imposed by the Supreme Court in the 1974 Detroit school case (*Milliken v. Bradley I*),[8] civil rights lawyers still seek metropolitan remedies in some large, predominantly black school districts. And most usually oppose suggestions that they consider alternative plans with less reliance on busing as the remedy for racially isolated schools.[9] Their strategy has the virtue of consistency. And there are some smaller districts, or large districts with relatively small minority population, where this strategy is perhaps defensible. But it becomes clear, particularly in the wake of the Supreme Court's refusal in 1977 to approve traditional school desegregation orders in Austin, Texas;[10] Omaha, Nebraska;[11] and Dayton, Ohio;[12] that judicial support for relief relying on racial balance has been greatly diluted and could disappear entirely. Based on their utterances in recent years, it appears that at least three members of the current Court, Chief Justice Berger and Justices Powell and Rehnquist, would not be displeased by such a disappearance.

In an oft-cited legal article written in 1959, Columbia law professor Herbert Wechsler criticized the Supreme Court's decision in Brown for failing to weigh the right of whites to nonassociation with blacks against the right of blacks, recognized in Brown, to attend the same public schools as whites.[13] While many legal scholars have sought to respond to Professor Wechsler's complaint, it remained true that the

Court in *Brown* had neither recognized nor evaluated any rights that whites had to sacrifice in order to make school desegregation possible. But in current decisions the Court is both recognizing and evaluating those rights. They are not designated as white rights of non-association but rather as interests in local control (*Milliken* v. *Bradley I*),[14] or "local autonomy of school districts" reflecting a "vital national tradition" (*Dayton*).[15] Attending a neighborhood school is now a recognized interest which district courts are instructed to balance against relief requiring racially balanced schools.

Courts will usually enjoin governmental policies where their major purpose is the invidious discrimination against racial minorities. They will not generally invalidate equally harmful policies that serve a socially acceptable goal or further interests not overtly invidious. This dichotomy in school desegregation litigation is reflected in the Supreme Court's refusal to abandon its de jure–de facto distinction, that is, only school systems where the racial separation is the result of official action or policy (de jure) can be required by the Constitution to desegregate. Schools where racial separation of students is caused by neighborhood patterns or other factors not influenced by school officials (de facto) are not required by the Constitution to reduce or eliminate the racial isolation but may do so voluntarily. The courts have generally upheld such voluntary plans against court attacks by white parents.

In recent cases the Supreme Court has insisted that school systems be held accountable for only that degree of racial isolation attributable to board policies intended to have that result. Both the Fifth Circuit (Austin) and the Eighth Circuit (Omaha) have responded to Supreme Court remands with decisions indicating their compliance with the high Court's strict liability standards.[16] But the Supreme Court is likely trying to communicate, albeit not too coherently, that whatever the board's intention, if its policies furthered interests in local school autonomy or other legitimate educational goals, then those policies, even if they had a segregative effect, do not justify judicially ordered school desegregation remedies relying on racial balance and requiring extensive busing.

Over the years there has been an interesting and little-recognized reversal of litigation rules and strategies by lawyers for school boards and those representing plaintiffs. When the school desegregation cases were argued in the early 1950s, civil rights lawyers took a "realist" position toward the law, urging that the court's decision should reflect contemporary factors that had occurred since the "separate but equal" rules were adopted. The school board lawyers, on the other hand, took a "formalistic" position. They argued that their clients had, in good faith, relied on the "separate but equal" doctrine, and that it should not be changed.

Summing up his argument along these lines, the famous lawyer John Davis argued for the school boards that

> somewhere, sometime, to every principle comes a moment of repose when it has been so often announced, so confidently relied upon, so long continued, that it passes the limits of judicial discretion and disturbance.[17]

Lawyers for the black petitioners in the school desegregation cases asserted that the "separate but equal" rules should be abandoned and a new rule recognizing their clients' constitutional right to desegregated schools be adopted because of the clear harm and stigma attached to requiring their attendance at separate, usually inferior schools solely because of their race. School officials did offer arguments based on educational differences, safety, health, and preservation of public peace and order, but they were never able to explain why not even one black child could ever attend a white school. Thus their arguments really boiled down to, "Invidious or not, we want segregated schools."

The Supreme Court decided not even to legitimatize the school board position by balancing it against the interests of blacks in desegregation. But today there are no de jure segregated school systems in the overt, pre-1954 sense. In much current school litigation, it is the school board that asserts substantive, educationally rational reasons for not racially balancing their schools, while plaintiffs increasingly must take the position that racial balance is necessary even if expensive, disruptive, and educationally unproductive. In effect, plaintiffs are saying, "*Brown* is the law, and we want integrated schools without regard to the costs." A once-despised and still subordinated racial minority is not likely to succeed with a formalistic position that failed the southern states and their school boards twenty-five years ago.

There is a tendency to forget that the racial separation outlawed in the *Brown* case was but one manifestation of the racism which adversely affected minority children in segregated schools. The real evil was and is the persistent pattern of giving priority to the needs and interests of whites in a school system without regard to whether such priority pattern disadvantages blacks. Racially separate schools facilitated the white priority phenomenon, but its results can be achieved, often with great damage to minority children, within the structure of a desegregated school. Equally damaging is the exclusion of nonwhites from meaningful involvement in school policymaking, exclusion of nonwhite parents from active participation in their children's education on a day-to-day basis, and the inability of nonwhite parents to hold school personnel responsible for effective schooling of their nonwhite children. School remedies, particularly in large urban districts, should be addressed to all aspects of racism, not just separation. Those remedies should focus specifically on techniques intended to improve the educational effectiveness of schools where nonwhite children attend. Such emphasis is appropriate whether or not those schools are predominantly white.

The Supreme Court has indicated in a totally different context that the Constitution does not guarantee quality education. But that finding is irrelevant in litigation involving appropriate remedies for proven racial discrimination. If there were any doubt of this, the Supreme Court removed it in 1977 with its second decision in the Detroit school desegregation case.[18] There, the Court approved a Detroit school desegregation plan that rejected much of what racial balance was possible in the 80 percent black district in favor of a number of "educational components." These components included special courses in reading and communication skills, in-service training for teachers, vocational education programs, revised testing procedures, school-community relations and counseling and career guidance programs, cocurricular activities, bilingual and ethnic studies, and monitoring of school activities and policies by citizens' groups. The legal precedent in the Detroit case is valuable, but we need not be limited by its rather orthodox ideas regarding educational improvement, most of which were suggested by the Detroit School Board.

It is now possible to identify a number of public schools serving poor nonwhite children, and serving them in an educationally effective fashion. The components of this success—effective leadership, close parental involvement in the educational process, and accountable teachers—clearly indicate the character of educationally oriented relief which should be sought in future judicial decisions.

What courts need now are "equal educational opportunity" (EEO) plans containing these components. Flexibility should be emphasized to enable individual districts to pattern specified provisions to meet local conditions. If adopted by courts, these EEO plans could allay the generally held belief that the *Brown* mandate can only be met through racial balance techniques. Efforts should be made to convince private and government civil rights groups to adopt all or portions of EEO-oriented plans in current and proposed school litigation. School boards should also be approached, but the major emphasis should be placed on conveying an understanding of such plans to local minority groups and parents.

Minority children, to paraphrase the Goldwater campaign, need *Brown* today more than ever. There is no reason why its twenty-fifth anniversary should be a memorial service. It promised "equal educational opportunity" in 1954, and by focusing future efforts on educational effectiveness, we can utilize its still considerable precedental weight to move minority children closer to that goal. Only when urban black children in predominantly black schools are able to make satisfactory academic progress in those schools will racial integration schemes be able to attract whites to their schools. And not before then will such schools be able to provide on a truly peer basis the interracial benefits so desired by liberals.

NOTES

1. *Goss v. Board of Education*, 373 U.S. 683 (1963).
2. *Brown v. Board of Education*, 347 U.S. 483 (1954).
3. See Diane Ravitch, "The 'White Flight' Controversy," *Public Interest* 51 (1978): 135, 145–47.
4. Ibid.
5. Ibid.
6. Nancy St. John, *School Desegregation Outcomes For Children* (New York: John Wiley & Sons, 1975).
7. Ron Edmonds, "Advocating Inequity: A Critique of the Civil Rights Attorney in Class Action Desegregation Suits," *Black Law Journal* 3, p. 176.
8. *Milliken v. Bradley I*, 418 U.S. 717 (1974).
9. See D. Bell, "Serving Two Masters: Integration Ideals and Client Interests in School Desegregation Litigation," *Yale Law Journal* 85, no. 4 (March 1976): 470.
10. *Austin Indept. School District v. United States*, 97 S. Ct. 517 (1976).
11. *School District of Omaha v. United States*, 97 S. Ct. 2905 (1977).

12. *Dayton Board of Education v. Brinkman*, 97 S. Ct. 2776 (1977).

13. Herbert Wechsler, "Toward Neutral Principles of Constitutional Law," *Harvard Law Review* 73 (1959): 1.

14. *Milliken v. Bradley I*, 418 U.S. 717 (1974).

15. *Dayton*, 97 S. Ct. 2776 (1977).

16. *United States v. Texas Education Agency*, 564 F. 2d 162 (5th Cir. 1977); *United States v. School District of Omaha*, 565 F. 2d 127 (8th Cir. 1977).

17. L. Friedman, *Argument* 215 (1969).

18. *Milliken v. Bradley II*, 95 S. Ct. 2749 (1977).

3

School Desegregation Can Succeed:
The Pennsylvania Experience

Homer C. Floyd

EXTENSIVE SCHOOL DESEGREGATION has been achieved in Pennsylvania as a result of the efforts of the Pennsylvania Human Relations Commission to enforce the provisions of the Pennsylvania Human Relations Act.

Between 1968, when the commission initiated efforts to eliminate racial segregation and discrimination in the schools of Pennsylvania, and the 1977–78 school year, the commission was successful in bringing about desegregation in more than twenty school systems across the state, taking more than a hundred twenty thousand pupils out of a segregated status.

School desegregation in Pennsylvania has been unique in several respects. Pennsylvania is one of only a few states in which the impetus to desegregate schools has come from state action (rather than suits filed in federal court), and Pennsylvania is the only state in which the agency initiating the action is a human relations commission (rather than a state department of education).

However, throughout this process the commission has had the cooperation and support of the Pennsylvania Department of Education, which has joined the commission in requesting local school districts to desegregate and has worked with the commission in evaluating the desegregation plans which have been submitted. Furthermore, the standards by which school desegregation plans are evaluated were developed jointly by the commission and the Department of Education.

These standards are "Desegregation Guidelines for Public Schools," published March 29, 1968, and "Recommended Elements of a School Desegregation Plan," published May 15, 1968.

The "Guidelines" say that insofar as possible, every school building should reflect in its enrollment a cross section of the entire community. They also say that desegregation is a local responsibility and urge that local school boards involve the community in the preparation of desegregation plans.

"Recommended Elements" is a list of eleven questions that should be answered about every desegregation plan to determine how well it achieves its purpose. The commission and the Department of Education use "Recommended Elements" in evaluating school district desegregation plans submitted for approval. Although "Recommended Elements" includes questions about staff, in-service training, and curriculum, the crucial question with respect to pupil desegregation is

How nearly does the desegregation plan bring the percent Negro pupils in each building to within 30 percent of the percent Negro pupils among the buildings of the same grade span?

In other words, the "Recommended Elements" permit considerable flexibility in the assignment of pupils to a school. For example, in a school system where the percentage of black pupils in the elementary grade span is 40 percent, the ideal proportion of black pupils in every grade school in the district would be 40 percent. However, the allowable variance of 30 percent plus or minus means that an elementary school in that district may have as few as 28 percent black pupils $(30\% \times 40\% = 12\%; \ 40 - 12 = 28)$ or as many as 52 percent black pupils $(30\% \times 40\% = 12\%; \ 40 + 12 = 52)$ and meet the standard contained in the "Recommended Elements."

In the process of desegregating schools during the past years, the commission has worked with a number of local school districts which have submitted and implemented desegregation plans on a voluntary basis, as well as dealing with other school districts in which extensive litigation has been necessary.

Accordingly, the commission's experiences in school desegregation have been both voluminous and varied, ranging from small cities to metropolitan areas, from attitudes of complete cooperation to extreme resistance, and encompassing every degree of change from minimal adjustment to complete restructuring of a school district to produce quality integrated education for all of the pupils in the system.

There is evidence that the commission's desegregation efforts have helped black children academically. Superintendent Harry R. Faulk of the McKeesport Area School District made the following statement about desegregation in his system:

> The same (black) students in an integrated school had an average achievement of over nine months in a school year as compared to an average achievement of six months in a school year in a predominantly black school. These data tend to support the premise that black students achieve better in an integrated school than in a racially segregated school.

By "average achievement" Dr. Faulk was referring to the average of the gains in academic skills such as reading of these desegregated black pupils. In other words, these minority youth learned more in the classroom setting of black and white pupils learning together than in the racially isolated setting of predominantly one race. The benefits of desegregation are not just in terms of living-together skills but are also in terms of what are labeled the basics of education, the three Rs.

With regard to concerns about the progress of white students in desegregated schools, Superintendent Faulk added:

> We have now completed two years of operation as a racially balanced school system. Our test results show that the achievement of the white students did not suffer as a result of racially balancing the schools.

The superintendents of schools in both Harrisburg and York, in testimony before legislative committees, presented similar reports on the success of school desegregation in their districts. Six years after the schools of Harrisburg were desegregated, a report by Superintendent Benjamin Turner stated that reading scores on the Stanford Achievement Test had improved since desegregation. Children in the first three grades who began their education in a desegregated system were reading at levels two months above the national norm. Children in the higher grades who did not attend the school district's pre-kindergarten early childhood centers did not show as much improvement as the younger children but were reading at higher levels in 1976 than students in these grades in 1975, at each grade level from fourth through eighth grade. In this same period, the percentage of students reading at below average levels also decreased in eleven of the twelve grade levels.

Reporting in the *New York Times* in September 1976, Tom Wicker said that the test results from Harrisburg proved exactly what the U.S. Civil Rights Commission had stated in a recent report: that 82 percent of school districts have desegregated without serious disruption and with little variation in the rate of white flight between districts that desegregated and those that didn't.

While desegregation has been carried out and has worked well in small and medium-size cities in Pennsylvania, it has not been accomplished in the state's two biggest cities, Philadelphia and Pittsburgh. In both cities the desegregation effort has been enmeshed in legal proceedings during most of the ten years since the commission requested the school boards in the two cities to desegregate their schools. It is disappointing but understandable that the greatest problems in trying to desegregate schools would occur in the state's two metropolitan areas where the largest numbers of blacks and other minority group students attend school and where school boards face other major problems in financing and operating public school systems.

However, the difficulty of desegregating schools in large metropolitan areas and the elusiveness of the final goal of providing all children with a quality integrated education should not be considered reasons to abandon the goal of school desegregation, as would appear to be the suggestion of Dr. Derrick Bell, Harvard Law School professor who presented the keynote address at the 1978 conference in Philadelphia on which this book is based.

Dr. Bell notes the many problems and setbacks associated with efforts to desegregate schools in large urban areas and recommends consideration of a new strategy in which the emphasis would be on improving the educational effectiveness of schools where nonwhite children attend rather than on racial desegregation of such schools.

To support his position, Dr. Bell pointed to studies which he said showed that many minority students attending desegregated schools have not experienced educational gains, and to the fact that efforts to desegregate schools in large urban areas through traditional techniques have sometimes led to white flight and an increase in the percentage of black and other minority-group children in metropolitan school systems.

In short, Dr. Bell said that the goal of *Brown* v. *Board of Education* has been largely unfulfilled and that government and private civil rights groups should stop chasing the illusive goal of school desegregation and turn instead to efforts to improve the quality of education blacks are receiving in black schools.

To abandon the goal of school desegregation would be a serious mistake for many reasons, including the fact that Dr. Bell's proposed alternative is not well worked out and would be limited by many of the same factors that limit the success of traditional school desegregation efforts. But the main argument against abandonment of traditional school desegregation efforts is that many school desegregation plans have been devoid of the educational components necessary for quality education, and there are no assurances that the problem would be overcome by Dr. Bell's alternative suggestion.

In many cities, school districts have had to be sued to produce a desegregation plan in the first place, which means that they were not committed to the goals of desegregation. After losing the court suit or discrimination case, most such districts have made plans for minimum compliance with desegregation orders rather than for maximum results. Such plans usually provide only for student movement to accomplish certain numerical ratios and do not incorporate the additional components usually associated with quality education. Because of their basic lack of commitment to the goals of desegregation, many school administrators have no commitment to implement a desegregation plan successfully, and their performance as administrators rarely is judged by the manner in which they implement desegregation plans. They can drag their feet, even scuttle a desegregation plan, and still be rated as good administrators. In short, accountability for successfully implementing desegregation plans rarely is included in the job specifications for a school superintendent. Where desegregation plans involved substantial busing, the bus ride usually was equated with whether the students who were bused showed any improvement in terms of educational accomplishments. Critics of busing for desegregation say, "Look at all this busing and there's no change in the achievement scores of the students involved." They completely overlook the fact that busing is only transportation and has nothing to do with what happens inside the classroom.

When we seek to assess what has been accomplished in school

desegregation we find, first of all, that we have never identified those elements of a quality education which relate specifically to desegregation. As a result, any such assessment is suspect before we have identified the important components.

Secondly, we haven't focused on the ways in which school administrators and teachers may improve the curriculum to insure a quality education in a desegregation environment. We haven't identified the training needs of professional and nonprofessional staff of schools for effective operation of a desegregated school. There has not been much exploration of major intergroup issues in desegregation and urban programs, and related programs in personal interaction. Any effective education must be culturally based, with the teacher understanding the culture and the psychic background of the pupils. A teacher must understand how black pupils have been affected by racism and how they react to various stimuli. Multicultural and multiethnic education has not been but must be accorded a prominent place in the curriculum of teacher-training institutions. In addition to measuring a teacher's knowledge of his or her subject matter, educators must find a way to measure a teacher's ability to transmit skills and knowledge in terms of interpersonal relationships. A teacher must be able to know and experience the meaning of being black, of being poor, of growing up in a big city. The teacher must be able to sense the reactions of pupils and to feel the nuances of words and situations that have different meanings to people in different cultures. Such training and understanding would help teachers avoid stupid questions: "Why do you call yourself black when your skin is light brown?"

There have been a few notable exceptions, but in most school desegregation situations these factors were not taken into consideration and it is no great wonder that better results were not accomplished.

If real progress in learning can occur through interaction in an educational program, why should we not work on those issues in a desegregated environment rather than accept as an operating principle an ill-defined concept called quality education in black schools, with all the limitations of such a monolithic environment?

Furthermore, if civil rights leaders opt out on the issue of school desegregation, it will relieve pressure on society to desegregate in other areas beyond education. We can ill afford any such relaxation of efforts to combat racism in employment, housing, and other places of public accommodation.

The great need at this time is to better identify the components of quality education in a desegregated school and to work to improve results in these areas—not to accept racial segregation as a principle on which to try to build education in a democratic society.

4

Pluralistic Education— Beyond Racial Balancing

Irving M. Levine

ON JUNE 27, 1977, the Supreme Court handed down its second decision in the *Milliken v. Bradley* case.[1] It was the culmination of seven years of litigation over segregation in the Detroit public school system. The existence of segregation was established at the outset and the importance of the case lies in a number of features unusual in desegregation litigation.

For instance, busing children to achieve racial balance, while highly inflammatory, was more often ordered by the courts than not as the single most effective way to achieve school desegregation and by extension to promote integrated education. In 1974, the Supreme Court in the first *Milliken* decision reversed a massive busing plan on the ground that its application would affect districts in which no violations had been found.[2]

The compromise finally accepted in the second Supreme Court decision featured a limited amount of busing within the Detroit school district in conjunction with a program of remedial educational measures designed by the school board and accepted by the original plaintiffs.

Another unusual aspect of the case involved sources of funding for that remediation. In June 1977, the Supreme Court in *Milliken II* endorsed a plan to remedy the situation in Detroit which called upon the state of Michigan to share in the cost of programs which went beyond pupil assignment and were designed expressly to counteract the effects of long-term segregation. The Court in fact adopted the principle of state aid to supplementary education and intergroup relations programs.

Third, the case was extraordinary also in that by the time it reached the Supreme Court for the second time, a long process of bargaining had brought the original plaintiffs into an alliance with their opposition. This circumstance was commented upon by Justice Powell, who said: "The Court's opinion addresses this case as if it were conventional desegregation litigation. . . . One has to read the opinion closely to understand that the case as it finally reaches us is wholly different from any prior case."

Once the massive busing option was lost in the earlier case, the national civil rights leaders who had initially supported Bradley joined their erstwhile opponents, the Detroit School Board, to force the state of Michigan to pay its share for a series of educational measures designed to eliminate the effects of segregation. This approach was known as the "educational components" strategy and is the main concern of this paper.

The Supreme Court itself recognized that it had "not previously addressed directly the question whether federal courts can order remedial education programs as part of a school desegregation decree."[3] But while warning that the Detroit case could not be taken as a blueprint for others, Chief Justice Burger mentioned favorably and in great detail a number of lower court decisions that introduced one or another plan for remedial education to combat the effects of prior discrimination and segregation. The court clearly wished to imply a firm direction toward appropriate remediation, following the direction in *Brown* that "in fashioning and effectuating [desegregation] decrees, the courts will be guided by equitable principles."[4]

The "educational components" strategy required that the state of Michigan fund four programs in particular: reading, in-service training, testing, and counseling and career guidance. But these components represented only a part of a larger plan of supplementary aids recommended by the Detroit school leadership in their total plan for achieving desegregation and integration. That plan spelled out a detailed agenda for qualitative changes in the classroom, in interethnic relations, in the total school culture, and in school-parent relations. This agenda is best described in the lower district court's description of educational measures crucial to the desegregation process:

In a system undergoing desegregation, teachers will require orientation and training for desegregation. Parents need to be more closely involved with the school system and properly structured programs must be devised for improving the relationship between the school and the community. We agree with the State Defendants that the following components deserve special emphasis: (1) In-Service Training; (2) Guidance and Counseling; (3) Student Rights and Responsibilities; (4) School-Community Relations Liaison; (5) Parental Involvement; (6) Curriculum Design; (7) Multi-Ethnic Curriculum; and, (8) Co-Curricular Activities. Additionally, we find that a testing program, vocational education, and comprehensive reading programs are essential. We find that a comprehensive reading instruction program together with appropriate remedial reading classes are essential to a successful desegregative effort. Intensified reading instruction is basic to an educational system's obligation to every child in the school community. Finally, the court finds that an effective court-oriented monitoring program is necessary for effective implementation of a desegregation plan to assure that delivery of educational services will not be made in a discriminatory manner.[5]

To assess correctly the full importance of both the substance and the coalition politics of the Detroit decision, we must perhaps go even further than we have yet dared in projecting a new approach to the definition of integration in schools. By rejecting large-scale busing to achieve racial balance and affirming instead the legitimacy of a broadside attack on educational deficiencies as part of the desegregation process, the Court may well have constructed a new basis for defining the qualitative features of the elusive words *school integration*. It is our view that the Detroit decisions have begun to clear the way for the implementation of a concept we have previously written about[6] and which we have called "pluralistic education."

Pluralistic education is best understood by the growth of the "return to your roots" phenomenon in American life. Pluralistic education is a necessary concomitant to what social scientists and historians are calling "the new ethnicity" and "the new pluralism." It accepts the need to establish racial justice but says that success can only come from winning white and other nonblack minority allies to the cause. It insists that if healthy group identity is necessary for nonwhites, it is also important for white ethnics and others. It contends that proper attention must be paid by American education to the many complexities of American diversity with black-white factors being of paramount importance, but not to the exclusion of other ethnic realities.

Pluralistic education can perhaps be said to exist when a school system adheres to a number of principles. These include:

1. A maximum of racial and ethnic mixing consistent with the demographic realities.
2. Policies that foster equal opportunity, including remedial help where past discrimination or exclusion has created individual and/or group disadvantage.
3. Positive individual and group experiences with others.
4. Healthy self-identity based upon knowledge and acceptance of one's own group identity.
5. Knowledge of the heritage and life-styles of other racial, ethnic, religious groups and development of personal skills for cross-cultural competency.
6. Utilization of the family as well as the school as a transmitter of healthy intergroup values.
7. Realization that the norms of American society are defined by group status, group identity, group conflict, and group succession.
8. Acceptance of the legitimacy of group negotiation on behalf of individuals and for communal interests, but nonacceptance of the doctrine of group rights.

How then do we make the transition from a worthy 1954 concept of black-white desegregation to a more appropriate and politically realistic multiethnic concept that matches the social and demographic realities of the 1980s? Can we make the transition to a recognition of other legitimate group agendas without losing sight of racial justice as the major ethnic priority? Can we do so without further fragmenting the nation into racial and ethnic categories? What tools exist to help us in this effort, particularly in the educational field, where so many programs initiated with hope and enthusiasm have failed?

There is significant legislation in the educational field on the national and on the state level which could better be used to promote "pluralistic education." Almost all of this legislation is attached to various levels of funding. In addition to legislation, the ethnic studies field has led to new curriculums which promote positive understanding of American diversity. There is no longer any excuse for schools to feel they do not have the equipment to introduce high-level programs in multiethnic and ethnic heritage studies.

As an example of the helpful educational aids now available, it would be hard to find a more useful document than the checklist at the end of the *Curriculum Guidelines for Multiethnic Education*, edited by James Banks and published by the National Council for the Social Studies[7] (see also chapter five). This guide not only is incisive in detailing classroom procedures but also goes to the heart of faculty training and school administration in pluralistic education. Moreover, it represents the work of a distinguished black educator and his associates who broke through an earlier and narrower non-white minority model into a full-fledged curriculum plan for genuine ethnic pluralism. This plan pays serious attention to the reality of white diversity and to group identity factors in Jewish, Italian, Polish, Greek, and other white ethnic groups. It offers over thirty detailed principles, goals, and programmatic suggestions.

The legislative framework is made up of a variety of laws that date from 1950s legislation on state levels calling for equal educational opportunity, to more recent legislation which gives aid to emotionally handicapped children. Other laws that can be usefully applied are the Emergency School Aid Act designed to implement school desegregation, remedial education deriving from the Elementary and Secondary Education Act; and additional resources could come from bilingual/bicultural legislation and from the Ethnic Heritage Studies Program Act.

In addition, court decisions on school desegregation and financial equalization are additional spurs. Administrative requirements for affirmative action complete the picture.

It would not be difficult for administrators, once they accepted the need for the new approach, to work with the tools now available, though they would be more likely to succeed if there were a deeper and wider consensus for "pluralistic education" than exists for more conventional desegregation approaches. We would still, however, need improved methods to verify that this latest plan is just not another way to circumvent racial integration.

Even before the "educational components" strategy was made a reality by the Detroit decision, such a plan for verification was presented. The plan called for the creation of an "integration index." It was presented by this author to a special National Education Association desegregation conference in New York in 1975 and to an ethnic heritage conference in Washington in 1976. On these two occasions, both black and white desegregation leaders reacted positively. Yet they despaired of the politics of ever getting a fair hearing for the index because of the polarization on busing. There was also much fear by blacks that a loss on busing meant the downfall of the desegregation and prointegration dynamic.

The "educational components" in the Detroit decision are remarkably similar to the variables of the proposed index. Thus the hailing by the civil rights community of the final Detroit decision mandating state aid to "educational components" may open up the use of an index based on these components as a new standard for integration.

As an illustration of this new acceptance, 250 black, Hispanic, and white ethnic educators and organization leaders met in Chicago in 1978 at a special conference on pluralistic education and endorsed the "components strategy" and the plan for an index which measured compliance.

The plan for the integration index was offered not just as an instrument to measure achievement but also as a device to help desegregation adversaries settle conflicts by encouraging community and ethnic bargaining over the relative importance of the various components. Further, the index would serve as a recipe of the vital ingredients for successful integration. How much of each ingredient and how to mix them would grow out of practice that was closely watched by the courts. Eventually a weighted index would evolve that would be given legal status through court orders which accepted the broader standards of the index as being in compliance with equal educational practices.

The outline for the proposed integration index, with a few minor modifications, was presented in Chicago as follows:

1. Maximum degree of physical desegregation consistent with the demographic realities of the district with the supplementary use of voluntary and magnet plans to achieve better mixing.
2. Both formal and informal short-term physically integrated educational experiences should be the norm between schools where racial and ethnic balancing is not feasible.
3. Use of multiethnic curriculums which promote healthy self-identity and foster positive intergroup learning.
4. Intensive teacher training in self-identity, ethnic heritage, and intergroup relations techniques.

5. Affirmative action hiring without quotas.
6. Transitional bilingualism-biculturalism.
7. Equal financing for all schools with supplementary funding for districts with more severe urban problems.
8. Parental involvement in the educational process.
9. Remedial education to be offered through the use of both professional and self-help mutual aid techniques.
10. Variable learning settings which have high achievement standards but which are diversely designed to mesh the culture of the educational experience with the culture of the home and the streets.
11. School-community relations programs to interpret the complexity of pluralistic education and to recruit strong community support.

An index which measured efforts to implement the above goals would give added assurances to those that still believe in a racially and ethnically integrated society that the schools which adhere to its principles were playing their part in furthering that ideal.

Until now we have too often sought solutions to desegregation that are mechanical and ineffectual. As a result, relationships between children of different racial and ethnic groups are at a very low level. If the learning atmosphere deteriorates further, we shall raise a new generation that may well be more bigoted than the last. Our failure to address the burdens mechanical desegregation places on the children involved was noted by the U.S. District Court of the Eastern District of Michigan in endorsing the educational components strategy of the Detroit School Board. The court said:

> In our analysis, we have been mindful that rigid and inflexible desegregation plans too often neglect to treat school children as individuals, instead treating them as pigmented pawns to be shuffled about and counted solely to achieve an abstraction called "racial mix." We are aware of the adverse educational and psychological impact upon black children compelled to attend segregated schools; to separate them from other children solely because of skin pigmentation is indeed invidious. But, although the resulting injury is great, the remedy devised should not inflict sacrifices or penalties upon other innocent children as punishment for the constitutional violations exposed. We must bear in mind that since those committing the grotesque violations are no longer about, any such punishment or sacrifices would fall upon the very young; it is the children for whom the remedy is fashioned who must bear the additional burdens.[8]

The true nature of the integrated society is really a complex arrangement of groups at different points on the spectrum between separatism and assimilation. Individual members of these groups vary greatly in their group loyalty and in their group-oriented behavior. Though the influence of group identity is often subtle, it should not be underestimated. Tribal feeling predominates at some stages of a people's development, but at other stages alliances, coalitions, and common core values are the norm. In a fluid society, the proper equation of separation and mixing is still to be determined; in a democratic society, conscious choice of the way one identifies with a group must remain an option. Upward mobility may best be fostered by both strong group identity and an equally strong desire to take advantage of the best in the constantly changing mainstream of the integrated society.

The integration index would acknowledge this fluidity. It would establish high standards but would allow for flexible formulas designed to reach those standards.

To succeed, the index would need the endorsement of key black and other ethnic leaders in the search for the best education for all children. As the conference in Chicago demonstrated, desegregation leaders, who have rightfully sought formulas for correcting the past wrongs of segregated schools, are asking themselves now whether an overreliance on the old racial balancing strategy can still be pursued with the same confidence that the end result will be better education and better intergroup relations. They may agree that a modified approach, which seeks to maximize both a substantial level of mixing and the quality of the mix, may now be timely. Moreover, since the many failures of school desegregation are casting the very idea of the integrated society into disrepute, those who still believe in integration as an ideal should now seek better means to further that ideal.

Now might be the moment for all who have been so long committed to the cause of racial justice and quality education to seek together the kind of grand compromise that combines the social justice and social idealism of *Brown* with the great practical wisdom of the Detroit decision.

Notes

1. 433 U.S. 267, 53 L. Ed. 2d 745, 97 S. Ct. 2749.
2. 418 U.S. 717, 41 L. Ed. 2d 1069, 94 S. Ct. 3112.

3. 433 U.S. 279.

4. *Brown v. Board of Education*, 348 U.S. 294, 300, 99 L. Ed. 1083, 75 S. Ct. 753, 57 Ohio Ops. 253, 71 Ohio L. Abs. 584.

5. 402 F. Supp., at 1118.

6. See Irving M. Levine, "A Proposal for the Creation of an Integration Index," Institute on Pluralism and Group Identity, New York, 1976; and David G. Roth, "A Pluralistic Index for School Desegregation," Institute on Pluralism and Group Identity, Chicago, 1976.

7. James A. Banks, ed., *Curriculum Guidelines for Multiethnic Education*, Position Statement (Washington, D.C.: National Council for the Social Studies, 1976).

8. 402 F. Supp., at 1118.

5

Teaching Ethnic Studies:
Key Issues and Concepts

James A. Banks

IN RECENT YEARS, vigorous efforts have been made by schools and colleges to implement ethnic studies programs. Most of these programs were created in response to demands made by ethnic minorities who felt that their cultures were distorted, omitted, or presented primarily from a white Anglo-Saxon point of view in the school curriculum. The earliest and most vigorous demands for ethnic studies programs came from Afro-Americans and were part of the Black revolt of the 1960's. Afro-Americans staged a fight for their rights in the 1960's which was unprecedented in their history. They tried to gain control of their schools and communities and to shape a new identity.[1] Keenly aware of the extent to which written history influences how a group sees itself and how others see it, Blacks demanded that Afro-American history be reinterpreted in ways that would enhance their image in the larger society and help their children to develop more positive self-concepts. They called for the inclusion of more Black heroes in school books and demanded that textbooks which they considered racist be banned from the public schools.

Other alienated ethnic minorities followed the pattern set by Afro-Americans and made similar demands for ethnic heritage programs which reflected their cultures, aspirations, and political goals. They also expressed ways in which they were oppressed by the larger society

The author is grateful to the National Academy of Education for support in the form of a Spencer Fellowship, which enabled him to research and write this article. The ideas in this article are further developed in the author's book, *Teaching Strategies for Ethnic Studies* (2d ed.: Boston: Allyn & Bacon, 1979).

and maintained that their plight in society was not taught in the schools. Chicano spokespersons called for a reinterpretation of the "winning of the West" and argued that the United States gained the Southwest ruthlessly by prodding Mexico into war in 1846 to seize its northwest territory. Consequently, they asserted, the Mexican-Americans were a colonized people within their native land.[2] American Indian leaders argued that they were the first and therefore the native Americans. They maintained that American history should be seen from an Indian or Native point of view.[3] Puerto Rican American writers stressed their colonial status and explained how Puerto Rico remained a colony when it came under American tutelage after the Spanish-American War ended in 1898.[4] Although less militantly than other groups, Asian American groups, such as Japanese Americans, Chinese Americans and Filipino Americans voiced their discontent with the way in which American history was taught in the schools. Some Japanese-American activists expressed outrage because they were dubbed the "model minority," and noted how the "success myth" was used to minimize and obscure the serious psychological problems and discrimination experienced by Japanese Americans. Chinese Americans highlighted the injustice of the Chinese Exclusion Act of 1882; Filipino Americans emphasized the racism and injustice which they experienced in California in the 1920's and their low socio-economic status in contemporary society.[5]

Some common threads ran through the complaints and expressions of these ethnic groups. Most of them stressed ways in which they were colonized peoples, victims of discrimination and White racism, politically powerless, and their need for ethnic heritage programs that would enhance their group's self-perceptions and contribute to their economic, political, and psychological liberation. The call for ethnic studies programs spread widely. White ethnic groups, such as Polish Americans, Italian Americans, and Irish Americans, demanded ethnic studies programs that would focus on their particular ethnic groups.[6] In some communities White ethnic groups and nonwhite minorities aggressively competed for limited resources allocated for ethnic studies programs. Many nonwhite ethnic minorities interpreted the efforts by White ethnics to establish ethnic heritage programs as another form of racism designed to divert attention from the serious plight of oppressed and alienated minorities. Intense conflicts among these factions emerged in some urban school districts.

CURRENT ETHNIC STUDIES PROGRAMS

The types of ethnic studies programs which have been formulated in most school districts and colleges reflect the political and social demands that have been made within local communities. Largely responding to crises and public pressure, curriculum specialists have devised ethnic studies programs without giving serious thought to the basic issues which should be considered when curriculum changes are made. The nature of learning, the broad social and psychological needs of students, and the structure of knowledge are types of problems and issues which received little if any consideration in the hurriedly formulated ethnic studies programs which now exist in many schools and colleges. Rather the overriding consideration was to create some kind of program so that demands would be met and militant ethnic students and faculty would be silenced. Consequently, most of the ethnic studies programs which have been devised and implemented are parochial in scope, fragmented, and structured without careful planning or clear rationales. Typically, school ethnic studies programs focus on one specific ethnic group, such as Puerto Rican Americans, Afro-Americans, or Native Americans. The ethnic group upon which the program focuses is either present or dominant in the local school population. In schools which are predominantly Mexican American there are usually courses in Chicano studies but no courses or experiences which will help students to learn about the problems and heritages of other ethnic groups, such as Afro-Americans, Filipino Americans, or Jewish Americans.

SPECIALIZED ETHNIC STUDIES COURSES

Ethnic studies programs which focus on one ethnic group have merit and can serve several useful purposes. Most ethnic minority students are quite ignorant about their histories and have learned many damaging and self-destructive myths about their peoples from textbooks, teachers, and the larger society. Some research suggests that many ethnic minority youths have deflated self-concepts and express low evaluations of their ethnic group.[7] Although it is romantic and unrealistic to expect ethnic content to work miracles on students' self-concepts and self-perceptions, ethnic minority youths have a right and a need to learn about their heritages before they are exposed to content about the cultures of other groups. Individuals who do not know, accept, and understand themselves rarely have the capacity to understand and empathize with others. Thus specialized ethnic heritage courses will remain necessary as long as ethnic minorities have unique intellectual, psychological, and political needs, and are excluded from participation in the larger society. Often minority group students need to ponder their destiny, plan strategies, soul search, and engage in self-criticism. Specialized ethnic studies courses and experiences can and do function to satisfy the unique needs of students who belong to victimized and excluded ethnic minority groups.

ETHNIC MODIFICATION OF THE TOTAL CURRICULUM

However, curriculum specialists have rarely seen the need to go beyond such specialized courses, which are almost always electives, to modify the entire curriculum with ethnic content and experiences. In this essay, I am concerned primarily with the need for changing the total curriculum so that it reflects the role of ethnicity in American life and validly describes ethnic cultures in our society. If such a task is deemed desirable, and I feel strongly that it is, then specialized ethnic heritage courses are grossly insufficient. Such courses are usually not found in predominantly White schools; they tend to emphasize isolated facts about shadowy ethnic heroes; and they do not help students develop valid comparative concepts and generalizations about ethnicity in the United States. They are based on the intellectually indefensible assumption that only ethnic minorities need to study ethnic minority history and culture.

We need to make some different assumptions about ethnic studies programs, to broaden our working definition of ethnicity, and to design ethnic studies programs so that they reflect contemporary sociological findings and current research and theory about the nature and acquisition of knowledge. All students in American public schools need to develop a minimal level of ethnic literacy and to understand the role of ethnicity in American life.[8] White students, whether they live in a wealthy New York suburb or in the heart of Appalachia, should know something about the pain and suffering experienced by Native Americans when they were pushed from east of the Mississippi to Indian Territory[9] in the 1800's and about the shocking and dehumanizing internment of Japanese Americans during World War II. Afro-American students, as well as Puerto Rican Americans, ought to know that, when the Statue of Liberty was dedicated in 1886, nativism directed against Southern and Eastern European immigrants and Catholics was rampant in the United States, and that Emma Lazarus' poetic words, "Give me your tired, your poor," fell on deaf ears.

Except for the important contributions of the first Americans and native Mexicans, American institutions were created by the sweat and toil of diverse peoples from foreign nations, most of whom were searching for a promised land. Because of the ways in which American society evolved, students cannot understand the complexity of American history without studying about the ways in which ethnic conflicts and struggles influenced its development. Most students study American history, yet few of them are exposed to ethnic content in any meaningful way. School history consists primarily of the agreed-upon myths which are perpetuated by the school and the larger society. Ethnic content, such as facts about the Mexican-American War and the Spanish-American War, if looked at from the points of view of Chicanos and Puerto Rican Americans, will shatter many romantic myths about the United States and reveal the extent of American imperialism and racism in the late 19th century.

AN EXPANDED DEFINITION OF ETHNICITY

Reconceptualizing and broadening the working definition of ethnicity will facilitate the development of ethnic studies programs and experiences which are more consistent with current sociological research and learning theory. Most curriculum specialists have equated an ethnic group with an ethnic minority group, and have consequently considered ethnic minority studies ethnic studies. Ethnic studies and ethnic minority studies should be distinguished. We can clarify the differences between these two types of programs by distinguishing between an ethnic group and an ethnic minority group. Individuals who constitute an ethnic group share a sense of group identification, a common set of values, behavior patterns, and other culture elements which differ from those of other groups within a society. A sense of common identity is probably the most essential characteristic of an ethnic group. Glazer and Moynihan point out that ethnic groups in contemporary society are often economic and political interest groups.[10] If this sociological definition of an ethnic group is accepted, then all Americans are members of ethnic groups.[11] Not only are Italian Americans, Greek Americans and Polish Americans members of ethnic groups, but so are White Anglo-Saxon Protestants and Irish Americans.

Some highly assimilated White Americans may argue that they are not members of an ethnic group because they are descended from many different ethnic strains and do not consciously identify with any ethnic group or have ethnic characteristics. This type of argument is an unwitting indication that such individuals are culturally Anglo Saxons and members of the dominant ethnic group. They have acquired the values, aspirations, language, behavior, and norms of the dominant culture. Because a culture is dominant does not make it any less ethnic, although it may be perceived as non-ethnic because it is the ideal culture with which all others are compared and the standard by which levels of cultural assimilation are determined.

An ethnic minority group is an ethnic group with several distinguishing characteristics. Like an ethnic group, an ethnic minority group shares a common set of values, behavior patterns, and a sense of peoplehood. However, its members have unique physical and/or cultural characteristics which enable persons who belong to dominant ethnic groups to easily identify them and thus to treat them in a discriminatory way. Most ethnic minorities within a society are also politically and psychologically oppressed and constitute a numerical minority. Out of a total of 204 million people in the United States in 1970, there were approximately 22 million Afro-Americans, 5 million Mexican Americans, 1.5 million Asian Americans, 1.5 million Puerto Rican Americans, and 792,000 American Indians. All of these groups, except the Japanese and Chinese Americans, were at the lower rungs of the economic ladder. There were over a half million Cuban Americans in 1974. Jewish Americans are one of the most significant White ethnic minorities in the United States.[12]

BROADENING ETHNIC STUDIES PROGRAMS

The definition of ethnicity delineated in this essay suggests that ethnic studies programs must be expanded to include the experiences of a wide range of American ethnic groups, including White Anglo-Saxon Protestants, Irish Americans, Greek Americans, Italian Americans, as well as ethnic minority groups. Such an ethnic studies program would do more than accurately reflect the sociological meaning of ethnicity; it would enable students to develop high-level concepts, generalizations and theories about American ethnic groups, thus enabling them to become more effective decision makers in contemporary society. Researchers and curriculum theorists have pointed out that students must study more than one content sample or group in order to develop valid concepts and generalizations.[13] Conclusions derived using only one sample or group are mere summary statements. To formulate valid high-level generalizations about a concept such as immigration, students must consider the experiences of such diverse immigrant groups as French Huguenots in the 1600's, the Chinese in the 1860's, and Filipinos in the 1920's.

Broadly conceptualized ethnic studies have other advantages. Students are able to develop more sophisticated understandings of the complex nature of ethnicity in the United States when they compare and contrast the experiences of different ethnic groups. A student who only studies Native Americans and learns about such atrocities as the Sand Creek Massacre in 1864 and the Wounded Knee Massacre in 1890 might reach invalid conclusions about violence and ethnicity in America. Unless a student also studies about the widespread lynching of Afro-Americans around the turn of the century, about the 11 Italian Americans who were lynched in New Orleans in 1891, and about the 19 Chinese who were killed by a White mob in Los Angeles in 1871, he or she may conclude that the experiences of Native American groups bear little resemblance to that of other ethnic groups in the United States.

When students study ethnic cultures using a comparative approach, they can correctly conclude that no one ethnic group has alone been the victim of atrocities, racism, and dehumanization in America. However, when looking at ways in which various ethnic groups have been victimized, the teacher should avoid the "Who's had it the worst?" approach. This approach to a comparative study of the ethnic groups will result in superficial and simplistic learning by students. Individual and group responses to bigotry and oppression are too complex and diverse for these kinds of easy comparisons to be validly made.

However, sensitive and informed teachers can help students to reach valid generalizations when they are comparing the experiences of ethnic groups. For example, the French Huguenots, the Scotch-Irish, the Irish, as well as Italian Americans experienced much discrimination in America. However, rejection experienced by White ethnic groups has usually not been as extreme or permanent as it has been for non-white ethnics. When they have attained sufficient levels of assimilation and social mobility, Whites are usually permitted to join the mainstream. However, nonwhite groups, such as Afro-Americans and Mexican Americans, are often excluded from participation in the larger society even when they have become culturally indistinguishable from the most acculturated Anglo-Americans. When students study about problems of acculturation and assimilation, the teacher should point out that both White and nonwhite ethnic individuals who become highly assimilated pay a tremendous psychological and personal cost for denying their ethnic heritages and acquiring one which is in many ways "foreign." The nonwhite individual's problems are especially acute since he or she is not accepted by the group whose cultural characteristics he or she has acquired.

A CONCEPTUAL APPROACH TO ETHNIC STUDIES INSTRUCTION

Ethnic studies programs should focus on higher levels of knowledge so that students can understand the complex nature of ethnicity in contemporary society. In many ethnic studies programs emphasis is placed on factual learning and the attainments of ethnic heroes. These types of programs use ethnic content but what Cuban has called "White instruction," or traditional teaching methods.[14] Isolated facts about Crispus Attucks do not stimulate the intellect or increase students' intellectual abilities any more than trite facts about Thomas Jefferson or Betsy Ross. The emphasis in sound ethnic studies programs must be on concept attainment; facts should only be used to help students to master higher-level concepts and generalizations.[15]

Concepts taught in ethnic studies should be drawn from several disciplines. It is necessary for students to learn to view ethnic events and behavior from the perspectives of several disciplines because any one discipline gives them only a partial understanding of intergroup and intragroup problems. When students are trying to determine what factors cause race riots, they will need to view riots from the perspective of the historian, the political scientist, the economist, and the psychologist, as well as from the point of view of the riot participant. In the remainder of this essay several key concepts which can enrich ethnic studies teaching are discussed. They are drawn from several disciplines.

CULTURAL AND STRUCTURAL ASSIMILATION

Each of the social science disciplines uses key concepts which can help students to better understand the relationship between behavior and ethnic group membership. Cultural assimilation, a concept used frequently by anthropologists and sociologists, is extremely useful in studying behavior related to ethnicity. When a member of an ethnic group acquires the behavior patterns, life styles, values, and language of the dominant group, he or she is culturally assimilated. Cultural assimilation is the process by which an individual or group acquires the culture traits of a different ethnic group. Since the dominant ethnic group controls most of the social, economic, and political institutions in society, members of ethnic minority groups must acquire its cultural traits to move up the social and economic ladder. When studying this concept it is very important for students to learn that although nonwhite ethnic minorities may become totally assimilated culturally, they will still be victims of discrimination and racism because of their different physical characteristics.

Gordon, in a perceptive and influential book, makes a useful distinction between cultural and structural assimilation.[16] While a group which has culture traits similar to the dominant ethnic group is culturally assimilated, an ethnic group is structurally assimilated only when it can and does participate in the primary social relationships of the dominant group, such as their private clubs and social cliques. While there is a high degree of cultural assimilation in American society, it is structurally pluralistic because many ethnic groups confine their primary social relationships to their own ethnic group, both because they are often excluded from other groups and because they often prefer to socialize with people like themselves. Highly culturally assimilated Japanese Americans often marry within their ethnic group, belong to Japanese social and cultural organizations, and participate in other ethnic activities.[17] Together, these two concepts can help students to understand why many highly acculturated Afro-Americans and Mexican Americans confine many of their activities to their ethnic communities.

IMMIGRATION–MIGRATION

Immigration and migration, concepts usually associated with history and geography, can also enrich ethnic studies instruction. During their study of the immigration and migration of ethnic groups students can profitably compare and contrast the reasons why the various groups immigrated and the kinds of experiences which they had in America. The special case of African immigrants to America should be highlighted. Africans differed from all other immigrant groups because their immigration was forced. They were also the only immigrant group enslaved upon their arrival in the Americas. All of the other immigrants voluntarily came to America.[18] When studying about the Southern and Eastern European immigrants to the United States, students can note how each of these groups experienced discrimination, lived in urban ghettos, and how many of them eventually became culturally assimilated, attained social mobility, moved to the suburbs, and began to oppress nonwhite ethnic groups. Groups like Italians and Poles discriminated against Afro-Americans and Mexican Americans when these groups started migrating to large cities after the two great world wars.

While European immigrant groups, especially those from Southern, Central, and Eastern Europe, were often the victims of racist ideologies, the racism[19] which they experienced never reached such alarming proportions as it did on the West Coast when Asian immigrants arrived there in the 1800's or in the South against Afro-Americans after the Civil War. It is important for students to realize that while certain classes of European immigrants, such as lunatics, convicts and those likely to become public charges, were prevented from entering the United States in the 1800's, the first national group that was totally excluded from the United States was nonwhite. The Chinese Exclusion Act of 1882 completely stopped Chinese immigration to the United States. By studying American immigration policy from 1882 to 1952 students will discover that there was a deliberate policy to keep this nation both White and Anglo-Saxon.[20]

NATIVISM

Students need to examine nativistic movements in the United States so that they can understand why rejection of out-groups is not always related to racial differences.[21] As early as 1727 negative feelings toward the Germans in Pennsylvania ran high. In 1792 Congress passed the Alien and Sedition Acts partly to harass European immigrants. Anti-foreign attitudes and movements ebbed and flowed up to the late 1800's. Nativism grew increasingly strong as the fear of a Catholic takeover of the federal government and of foreign "radicals" soared in the 1880's. The big jump in the number of Southern and Eastern European immigrants entering the United States in the 1880's added fuel to the fire. Cries of "100% Americanism" and "America for Americans" became salient. Agitation for antiforeign legislation became intense, especially legislation that would exclude foreign "radicals" and require immigrants to pass a literacy test. The proposed literacy test was designed to eliminate immigration from Southern and Eastern Europe.

Nativistic movements, which were directed against most foreign-born groups in the 1850's, began to focus increasingly on Southern and Eastern European immigrants as masses of them continued to arrive in American cities. Writers, like the Jensens and Shockleys of today, legitimized the widespread racist myths about the innate inferiority of Southern and Eastern Europeans. In 1899, William Z. Ripley published *The Races of Europe* in which he divided Whites into three major races and warned against the biological mixing of inferior and superior White races. He judged the Teutonic the superior race. Madison Grant, a naturalist, set forth a similar argument in *The Passing of the Great Race in America*, published in 1916.

Eventually the nativistic forces gained congressional victories. A comprehensive immigration bill was enacted in 1917 which established a literacy test for entering immigrants and extended the classes of those excluded. When the literacy test failed to reduce significantly the number of Southern and Eastern European immigrants, nativists pushed for more restrictive legislation. They succeeded in 1921 when the Johnson Act was passed. This act, which marked a turning point in American immigration, set up a nationality quota system and imposed the first numerical limits on immigration from European nations. Finally, the Johnson-Reed Act was enacted in 1924. The quotas set up by this act were severe and blatantly discriminated against Southern and Eastern European and nonwhite nations. The act completely stopped Japanese immigration. The Immigration Act of 1924 marked the triumph of nativistic forces and closed a significant chapter in American history.

POLITICAL REFUGEES

Fortunately, the story of American immigration does not end with the Johnson-Reed Act of 1924. More humanistic gestures were made by American policymakers in subsequent years. When Communist revolutions occurred in a number of foreign countries in the post–World War II period, the United States served as an asylum for citizens of these nations who were displaced or who felt that the political developments in their countries were intolerable. These aspects of immigration must be taught so that students will gain a total perspective on American immigration policy. In 1948 a Displaced Persons Act was passed which permitted about 400,000 refugees to enter the United States. Five thousand Hungarian immigrants entered the United States under the terms of a Refugee Relief Act passed in 1954.

A study of refugee immigrants can lead to an examination of the status and history of one of the most recent immigrant groups in the United States, Cuban Americans. After Castro came to power in 1959 thousands of Cubans fled to the United States. Today there are nearly a half million Cuban Americans in the United States, located mainly in Miami, Florida. A significant number also live in New York City. In 1965 the United States began a Cuban Refugee Airlift program to help Cuban refugees reach the United States.

Students can compare the attitudes of Cuban Americans with those of other Spanish-speaking groups in the United States. They will discover some interesting differences. Most Cuban Americans are staunchly anticommunist, politically conservative, and regard the United States as an asylum which enabled them to escape from an oppressive government. On the other hand, militant Mexican Americans and Puerto Rican Americans feel that the United States is an imperialistic oppressor of colonized peoples. An examination of the immigration act of 1965, which abolished national origin quotas and greatly liberalized American immigration policy, will also help students to understand and appreciate the fact that there are both liberal and oppressive forces in American society.

CULTURAL VALUES

When students study ethnic cultures, major emphasis should be given to the core values within the various cultural groups. Values, like attitudes and beliefs, are learned from the groups in which the individual is socialized; we are not born with a set of values and do not derive them independently. While there are some broad and general values embraced by most American communities (such as respect for the lives of those regarded as human and kind treatment of children), these general values are often defined and perceived differently within various ethnic subcultures, or they take diverse forms. Other values are very important in some ethnic communities and largely absent from others.

The Nisei[22] usually endorse many traditional Japanese values, including etiquette, personal control, the samurai ethic, a high respect for authority, the achievement ethic and a strong sense of family obligation.[23] Family obligation in traditional Japanese cultures was often considered much more important than personal freedom. Although many of the Nisei values have eroded among the Sansei because the Sansei are highly culturally assimilated, important vestiges of these values remain in Japanese communities today, especially among the elderly. Some of these values such as high respect for authority and a strong sense of family obligation conflict with dominant Anglo-American norms. In Anglo society there is often little respect for authority and it is rarely concentrated in one family member.

Values in other ethnic minority communities are often different from those in Anglo society. In the traditional Puerto Rican family the girl was highly protected and the father was the undisputed head of the family. The family was also a highly interdependent unit. Uncles, aunts, and other relatives were often considered an integral part of the family unit. This type of extended family was also common among Afro-Americans in the deep South. As Afro-Americans and Puerto Rican Americans become more urbanized and more heavily represented in the middle classes, these aspects of their cultures diminish. However, the extended family is still very much a part of these ethnic cultures. Puerto Rican girls in East Harlem often do not have the same freedom to come and go with boys as their Anglo peers.[24]

When American Indians are studied in school, students are usually introduced to certain stereotypic components of their cultures such as tepees, baskets, canoes, or moccasins. While these tangible elements were part of the cultures of some Native American groups, they were by no means the most essential part of them. Thus students gain only a superficial and distorted view of Indian cultures when they only study tangible culture elements. The essence of a culture can be understood only by studying its central values and their relationships to the daily lives of the people.[25] The Native American view of humans and their relationship to the universe must be studied to understand traditional Indian values toward people and nature.[26] Indian groups tended to look upon the universe as a whole, with every object having a sacred life; to separate humans from nature was antithetical to the Great Spirit, for to the Great Spirit all was life. The native Americans felt that they existed in unity and in harmony with nature.

It is the values and related life-styles of ethnic communities which constitute their essence, and not chow mein, basket weaving, sombreros or soul food. These values should be emphasized in the curriculum, not exotic cultural elements whose major instructional outcome is the reinforcement of stereotypes. I am not suggesting that tangible cultural elements should not be studied, only that they should not be emphasized in the cultural studies. While the study of ethnic values should constitute a large part of an ethnic studies curriculum, it is important to realize that the values of American ethnic groups are changing, especially among ethnics who are urbanized. Ethnic minorities are becoming urbanized at a much faster rate than Anglos. It is also important to remember that highly assimilated and higher status members of ethnic minority groups may share few, if any, characteristics with their more humble brothers and sisters. Despite these caveats, ethnic values are endemic in American life. They add strength and diversity to our national culture. This significant message should be communicated to all students.

CONCLUSION

To develop ethnic literacy and acquire a sophisticated understanding of ethnic cultures in the United States, students must experience an ethnic studies curriculum which is broadly conceptualized, includes content from a wide range of American ethnic cultures, and reflects current learning theory and research. When ethnic studies is narrowly defined and conceptualized, students are likely to reach invalid and tenuous conclusions about ethnicity in American life. Students must also master higher level concepts and generalizations and view ethnic groups from an interdisciplinary perspective in order to formulate effective solutions to ethnic problems and become successful change agents in contemporary society. While each of the disciplines contains key concepts and generalizations which are helpful in ethnic studies instruction, some of which are discussed in this essay, any one discipline can give students only a partial understanding of ethnicity in the United States. Ethnic content can serve as an excellent vehicle to help students expand their conception of humanity and to better understand their own cultures. Educators should take decisive steps to devise ethnic studies curricula which will help create a society in which peoples of different cultures can live in harmony. Immediate action is imperative if we are to prevent extreme ethnic polarization and the total dehumanization of American society.

NOTES

1. See James A. Banks and Jean D. Grambs, eds., *Black Self-Concept: Implications for Education and Social Science* (New York: McGraw-Hill, 1972).

2. Rodolfo Acuña, *Occupied America: The Chicano's Struggle Toward Liberation* (San Francisco: Canfield Press, 1972).

3. Jack D. Forbes, "Teaching Native American Values and Cultures," in *Teaching Ethnic Studies: Concepts and Strategies*, ed. by James A. Banks (Washington, D.C.: National Council for the Social Studies 43rd Yearbook, 1973), pp. 201–225.

4. For a range of views on the Puerto Rican experience see Francesco Cordasco and Eugene Bucchioni, eds., *The Puerto Rican Experience: A Sociological Sourcebook* (Totowa, N.J.: Littlefield Adams, 1973).

5. Strongly worded Asian American views are in Amy Tachiki, Eddie Wong, Franklin Odo, with Buck Wong, eds., *Roots: An Asian American Reader* (Los Angeles: UCLA Asian American Studies Center, 1971).

6. Mark M. Krug, "Teaching the Experience of White Ethnic Groups," in Banks, ed., *Teaching Ethnic Studies*, pp. 257–277; Andrew Greeley, *Why Can't They Be Like Us? Facts and Fallacies About Ethnic Differences And Group Conflicts in America* (New York: Institute of Human Relations Press, 1969).

7. Marcel L. Goldschmid, ed., *Black Americans and White Racism: Theory and Research* (New York: Holt, 1970), pp. 15–85.

8. This point is further developed in James A. Banks, "Teaching for Ethnic Literacy: A Comparative Approach," *Social Education*, 37 (December, 1973), pp. 738–750.

9. The eastern part of present-day Oklahoma was set aside for Indian settlement when Indians were forced from the East in the 1800's because this territory was considered uninhabitable by whites. This region became known as Indian Territory. See Edward H. Spicer, *A Short History of the United States* (New York: D. Van Nostrand, 1969).

10. Nathan Glazer and Daniel P. Moynihan, *Beyond the Melting Pot: The Negroes, Puerto Ricans, Jews, Italians and Irish of New York City* (Cambridge: M.I.T. Press, 1970).

11. This definition is supported in Charles H. Anderson, *White Protestant Americans: From National Origins to Religious Group* (Englewood Cliffs, N.J.: Prentice-Hall, 1970), p. xiii.

12. These figures are based upon United States Bureau of the Census, *Statistical Abstract of the United States* (Washington, D.C.: U.S. Government Printing Office, 1971).

13. Hilda Taba, *Teaching Strategies and Cognitive Functioning in Elementary School Children*, Cooperative Research Bureau Project No. 2404, U.S. Office of Education, San Francisco State College, 1966.

14. Larry Cuban, "Ethnic Content and 'White' Instruction," *Phi Delta Kappan*, 53 (January, 1972), pp. 270–273.

15. James A. Banks (with contributions by Ambrose A. Clegg, Jr.), *Teaching Strategies for the Social Studies: Inquiry, Valuing and Decision-Making* (2d ed.: Reading, Mass.: Addison-Wesley, 1977).

16. Milton M. Gordon, *Assimilation in American Life: The Role of Race, Religion, and National Origins* (New York: Oxford University Press, 1964).

17. Harry H. L. Kitano, *Japanese Americans: The Evolution of A Subculture* (Englewood Cliffs, N.J.: Prentice-Hall, 1969), pp. 79–97.

18. Some individual European immigrants who were convicts or social outcasts were forced to immigrate to Colonial America. However, all European nationality groups came to America voluntarily.

19. *Racism* is used here because many social scientists divided Europeans into several races in the late 19th and early 20th centuries. See John Higham, *Strangers in the Land: Patterns of American Nativism 1860–1925* (New York: Atheneum, 1972), pp. 131–157.

20. Maldwyn Allen Jones, *American Immigration* (Chicago: University of Chicago Press, 1960) is an excellent general history of European immigration to America.

21. The best general study of American nativism is John Higham, *Strangers in the Land: Patterns of American Nativism 1860–1925* (New York: Atheneum, 1972).

22. *Issei, Nisei* and *Sansei* refer to the first, second and third generation Japanese Americans respectively.

23. An informed and scholarly discussion of Japanese American values is in Stanford M. Lyman, *The Asian in the West* (Reno: Desert Research Institute, 1970), Special Science and Humanities Publication No. 4, pp. 81–97.

24. Elena Padilla, *Up From Puerto Rico* (New York: Columbia University Press, 1958) is a perceptive anthropological study of a New York Puerto Rican community. It contains a useful discussion of values in the Puerto Rican American community.

25. Forbes, "Teaching Native American Values and Cultures," p. 202.

26. See Harold E. Driver, *Indians of North America* (2d ed. revised: Chicago: University of Chicago Press, 1969); and T. C. McLuhan, ed., *Touch the Earth: A Self-Portrait of Indian Existence* (New York: Pocket Books, 1971), p. 15.

6

Private Schools
and Urban Integration

Thomas Vitullo-Martin

AT A RECENT conference with New York City public officials, a noted professor of urban studies proposed a solution to the problem of increasing segregation of the city's schools: close the private schools. His proposal recalls a similar one when the Federal District Court in New York attempted to remedy school segregation in the Coney Island area of Brooklyn (*Hart* v. *Community School Board,* 1974).

The special master in the case then noted that 12,000 of the area's 29,150 school-aged children went to parochial schools. If those schools were closed, he argued, perhaps facetiously, the integration problem in the public school would be solved.

Closing the private schools, were he serious, would have been a costly way gaining very little for integration. The major nonpublic schools, Catholic and Hebrew, enrolled a large proportion of minorities. Catholics enrolled an estimated 45 percent Spanish-surnamed and black students, the Hebrew schools a high percentage of Russian and other non-English-speaking immigrants. Even though the Hebrew day schools were almost entirely white, their population was so heavily immigrant that only the most formulistic integrationists would have argued that their racial integration would have helped solve the problems of racial integration of blacks. The proposal would have destroyed two religious school systems, posed constitutional problems, and was eliminated from consideration. In the end, the court adopted a magnet school plan.

Both the proposals of the urban studies professor and the special master are interesting for what their proponents assumed without investigation. Neither group was concerned about integration within the private schools; both assumed there were few if any minorities in the private schools and that the private schools were segregating. Neither saw the private schools as fostering democratic goals, such as increasing opportunities for minorities or increasing racial integration in the city. Both saw private schools as obstacles to public school integration success and as weakening the public schools.

Do private schools all segregate in one way or another? If they do, how? If they all are guilty of segregation, it is by one of three approaches: as segregation academies, where both school officials and parents choosing the school intend racial segregation; as neutral private schools, where the school does not intend to segregate but the parents may; and as integrationist private schools, where both school and parents are neutral on the question of segregation or intend to integrate, but nevertheless the school's presence promotes public school segregation by attracting white students. This last possibility implies the mere existence of private schools is detrimental to integration. We should examine these assumptions to see if the evidence suggests that private schools are obstacles to public school integration.

Private schools enroll too many blacks, other minorities, and children from low-income families to be deliberately segregating on any large scale. The Bureau of the Census's 1975 Survey of Income and Education found that 10 percent of the 48 million elementary and secondary students in the United States attend private schools and that these schools enrolled a surprising proportion of lower-income and minority students. Counting only cash income for families (and not in-kind income such as subsidized rent), the survey found (1) that 6 percent of all students from families with incomes below $1,000 per year were enrolled in private schools; (2) that in the northeast and north central states, 9 percent of that group was in private schools; and (3) that nationally, 12 percent of elementary students from families with incomes below $7,500 were in private schools.

The National Center for Education Statistics (NCES) found that in 1975, 7.4 percent of all black elementary school students in the West are enrolled in private school, compared to 6.6 percent of all white children. Private schools are serving proportionately more blacks than whites in the West. NCES found that the enrollment of blacks in private schools more than doubled between 1970 and 1975 in that region. More than half the western states have higher proportions of minority students in their private than in their public schools. For example, New Mexico's private schools are 57 percent minority, compared to 48 percent minority in the public schools, according to a 1970 survey by HEW's Office of Civil Rights.

In 1975, 21 percent of all school-aged children in the United States were Spanish-surnamed or racial minorities. Of these about 13 percent were black. If private schools were, on the whole, deliberately segregating, they would enroll much lower percentages of minorities. How have they done? The two private school systems enrolling the greatest numbers of non-European minorities are the Catholic, which enrolls about 75 percent of all private-school students and 90 percent of all blacks in private schools, and the Lutheran (Missouri Synod), which enrolls about 4 percent of all private-school students and about 5 percent of all blacks in private schools. The Catholic system was 18 percent minority in 1976, and the percentage minority was increasing. It was particularly high in some Catholic dioceses: The Montgomery District schools of the Mobile Diocese were 63 percent black (and 59 percent non-Catholic) in 1974. The Birmingham Diocese, which includes all of Northern Alabama, was 43 percent black. The Catholic elementary schools of the District of Columbia were 77 percent minority in 1974. About half the elementary students of the New York diocesan system were Spanish speaking in 1977. In the Lutheran schools, 10 percent of the elementary and 18 percent of the secondary students are black, a greater percentage at the secondary level than in public schools. Black student enrollments in both Catholic and Lutheran schools are substantially higher than black membership in either church. Only about 1.5 percent of Catholics and 1 percent of Lutherans are black. The high percentage of minorities enrolled in private schools is not consistent with the belief that the schools are elitist or deliberately racially segregating.

However, there are a number of genuinely segregationist academies in the South and West and it is possible that these schools effectively segregate some very small number of students of local areas. According to the best available data, at least 18,000 of the 20,500 identifiable private schools have nondiscriminatory admissions policies. Only one organization of private schools in the United States is avowedly segregationist: the Southern Independent School Association, which claims only 375 member schools in nine Deep South states. There may be as many as 2,500 segregationist schools in the

United States, according to estimates by the Council of American Private Education and the U.S. Office of Education. A disproportionate number of these schools are quite small, however, so that although they represent perhaps 15 percent of all private United States schools, they enroll no more than 5 percent of the total private school population, or 225,000 students, out of the 4.8 million in private schools. The remaining 4,575 million children attend private schools which have adopted nondiscrimination policies.

Many of today's segregated academies were not in their origins private schools but were subterfuges created by state and local authorities to avoid the Supreme Court's desegregation orders. Many private schools in the South in fact led the resistance to segregation. A private school was the last to segregate: Kentucky's Berea College succumbed to the Black Codes requiring segregation of all private schools only after losing its case before the Supreme Court in 1908. After the Supreme Court's *Brown* decision in 1954 tore down the segregation laws, private schools were the first to desegregate voluntarily. New Orleans's Catholic system desegregated two years before the public system acceded to a court order to end its dual system. (In the interim, Catholic schools experienced some white flight to the public schools.) St. Louis Catholic schools' decision to desegregate broke the resistance of its public school board to desegregation. In Mobile and Birmingham, Alabama, in Lafayette, Louisiana, and in several other southern cities, private schools voluntarily integrated before the public integrated under court orders.

By providing a way out for parents who disagree with a public school integration plan, it is possible for private schools which are integrationist in their commitments to have a segregationist effect on a city, say the critics. Private schools are also guilty of, to use a commercial analogy, holding a large stock of white students, when the public schools need those students to integrate.

In most places, the private schools do not compete on racial policies. We have already seen that private schools enroll almost as great a proportion of low-income and minority students as public. They enroll disproportionate numbers of immigrant children. And we have seen that in many places where the public schools maintained dual systems, the private schools were the first to integrate. They were a moral force for integration, not a hindrance. In general, private schools draw from relatively compact neighborhood areas. They therefore resemble their neighborhoods in population characteristics, just as do the public schools. In their socioeconomic composition, private schools rarely differ sharply from public schools.

One exception is private boarding schools—and to a lesser extent, selective independent schools. By tradition, and because of their high expenses and high tuitions, these schools draw students from middle- and upper-income families. Often they are located in central cities and so appear to be white enclaves in the midst of minority public systems. The appearance is deceiving. To determine whether the schools are integrating or segregating, we must compare them, and the choice they offer, to the alternatives most actively considered by the parents who utilize those schools. A large proportion of these schools belong to the National Association of Independent Schools. The association members provide scholarship aid to 15 percent of their students and have a 7 percent minority enrollment. These schools are far more racially and economically integrated than public schools serving the same income-range parents. In the high median-income counties outside New Orleans, Chicago, San Francisco, Washington, and in large sections of the wealthy suburban districts outside New York, Philadelphia, and other major cities, only about 1 percent of public school enrollments are minorities, and these students tend to be concentrated in one or two of the county's school systems. The choice for the patrons of the independent schools is, most typically, one of a racially and economically integrated private school versus a racially and economically segregated public school. The rule that private schools reflect their communities applies to these schools as well. Independent schools in central cities tend to have much higher black and lower-income enrollments than those in suburban areas or in the countryside. But even the suburban independent schools have more blacks and lower-income families than the public schools in their own neighborhoods. In comparing the two types of schools in communities around Boston, we found that suburban private schools were more able to attract minorities through scholarship and other programs, whereas public schools found it difficult to reach outside their wealthy (and de facto segregated) districts for minorities. As a rule, the select private schools choose their student body for heterogeneity, and similar public schools never do.

There is a second flaw in the argument that private schools segregate the city: it neglects the role of the suburban public schools.

Close the private schools and that stock of white parents leaves for the suburbs; they do not stay in the city. Suburban public schools have stripped the cities of their white middle class. The select private schools—in fact all private schools in the cities—have helped keep middle-class parents in the central cities.

There are two kinds of competition affecting public central-city schools: one from the private schools serving the same neighborhoods, which I will call microcompetition; and the other from public schools serving suburban or outlying areas, which I will call macrocompetition. The microcompetition takes place over educational issues: religious instruction, pedagogical approach, class size and amenities, academic achievement record. The competition tends to encourage a variety of offerings in the neighborhood—the schools differentiate their markets—and tends to encourage improvements where the schools meet head on: the schools compete to outperform each other. As a benefit, the microcompetition permits parents to change schools without leaving the neighborhood or city, and so—especially in working-class and inner-city neighborhoods—helps sustain property values, the tax base, and the neighborhood structures. In this way the presence of the private schools aids the public, including its integration programs.

The macrocompetition takes place between public schools in different areas. But to choose, parents must move. Parents choose public schools, paying a kind of tuition in the form of a premium on the purchase price of their house, as well as through local taxes. In general, the better the reputation of the school, the more expensive the property. The competition separates students by income. Ironically, the movement of the wealthy to suburban systems is virtually required by federal taxation policy: the school expenses of public suburban schools are deductible from taxable income. Tuition to urban private schools is not deductible. That means a family in the 50 percent tax bracket must devote only about $3,000 to get schooling for their child costing $5,000 in suburban public schools (since the costs are also shared by those with no children in the schools); whereas the parent using private schools must devote $16,600 income to be able to generate the same $5,000 pupil expenditure. In the wealthiest public school district in the New York area, the schools spend $8,600 per pupil. Considered in another way, the tax policy in effect means that the federal government pays $6,200 of this bill—the amount of income tax the federal government forgoes collecting from families in the highest tax brackets when it permits the $8,600 to be deducted.

The federal government, through its income tax system, enormously and disproportionately aids the wealthy in public schools and underpins the most racially and economically exclusive schools in the country with its aid. Private schools advance the social and racial integration of metropolitan areas and help improve the educational opportunities of low-income and minority families, directly through their own school offerings and indirectly through their competitive effects on public schools in the central cities, and through their tendency to stabilize public school neighborhoods and improve their tax base.

7

Why Johnny Can't—
The Problem of State School Financing

Rochelle L. Stanfield

DOES JOHNNY, that eternal symbol of the school child, have the opportunity for an equal education? For more than a generation, this has been one of the nation's most emotion-filled questions.

In the past decade, a new dimension has been added to the already sensitive issues of education and civil rights—the economic question of how the wealth of Johnny's neighborhood affects the schooling he receives.

The root of the question is money: who should pay how much for financing public elementary and secondary schooling. But the subsidiary questions are all-important. What should the role of state governments be? How heavily should the schools rely on the local property tax? What formulas for equalization are equitable and politically feasible?

"Much more than equalization of school support is involved," said James A. Kelly of the Ford Foundation. "It is a very stable, very intricate equilibrium, fiscally and politically, having to do not only with school politics but with property tax burden, and those are pretty darn tough to change." Kelly is the Ford Foundation's program officer in public education and has been responsible for many of the studies that have led to far-reaching reforms in the past five years.

ACTION

The New Jersey legislature now is grappling with a complicated

References to "this year" refer to 1976.

reform measure that is tied in with a controversial state income tax bill. The legislature is under court order to act.

Kentucky took a few steps forward in March with an overhaul of its school aid formula. South Carolina has a somewhat similar measure pending before its legislature.

In all, 20 states have adopted major education aid amendments since 1971. But in most cases, only the concept has changed, with dollar reforms hoped for at a later date.

"The states have adopted new formulas, and this is real progress," said John J. Callahan, director of the Legislators' Education Action Project of the National Conference of State Legislatures. "When the states have these formulas developed *and* funded, that will be real reform."

FUTURE

The revolution in school finance is being fought primarily in the state courts and the state legislatures, with only an indirect and minimal federal role so far. It has recruited a mixed army of supporters, including state and local officials, parents, citizens groups and civil rights activists, economists and academics.

The school aid reformers are not sure where the current trends are leading. Some predict retrenchment, noting that the economy has slumped and that the relatively easy reforms have been accomplished. Others see more progress, pointing out that the courts remain active in this field and that the energy-rich states have surpluses with which to finance new reforms.

All agree, however, that the 1970s will be looked back on as the decade of school finance reform.

BACKGROUND

"This is not a national reform movement in the sense that there is a single policy objective," explained the Ford Foundation's Kelly. "In the broadest sense, of course, everyone wants a reduction of inequities and fairer distribution of taxes to the schools. But there are as many different sets of problems, as many customs and as many different approaches to reform as there are states."

ORIGINS

The problems of inequities that plague public school financing arose, ironically, out of an earlier attempt to be fair.

Formulas adopted in the 1920s to redistribute tax resources from the wealthy urban areas to the poor rural school systems "were gradually outmoded by demographic trends that redistributed population and economic activity," according to Joel S. Berke of the Educational Testing Service's Education Policy Research Institute in Washington, D.C.

Nevertheless, these decades-old formulas remain in use by most of the states, and by the 1960s had lost most of their value as devices for equalizing school spending among a state's towns and cities, Berke concluded in an article in the University of Chicago's February 1974 edition of *School Review*.

Because the formulas had been diluted and because state aid constituted such a small share of local school costs, a community's property valuation "repeatedly turned out to be the primary determinant of spending levels for elementary and secondary schools," Berke wrote.

SERRANO

The growing inequities led to a series of legal challenges that began in the 1960s, but school finance reform received its biggest boost on Aug. 30, 1971, when the California Supreme Court, in *Serrano v. Priest*, struck down the California school finance system as in violation of both the state and the federal constitutions.

"We are called upon to determine whether the California public school financing system, with its substantial dependence on local property taxes and resultant wide disparities in school revenue, violates the equal protection clause of the 14th Amendment," the court said. "We have determined that this funding scheme invidiously discriminates against the poor because it makes the quality of a child's education a function of the wealth of his parents and neighbors."

California's system was typical of most states. School districts with high property values could raise substantial sums at low property tax rates; poor school districts—even at high property tax rates—could not approach the per-pupil expenditures of the rich districts. The court found a 10,000-to-1 disparity in revenue-raising ability among the school districts in California.

California, like most states, provided two kinds of aid to public elementary and secondary education. A flat "foundation grant" went to every school district, making the rich districts richer while helping the poor districts only minimally. In addition, California distributed "equalization aid" in inverse proportion to the property-tax-raising ability of the school districts. However, the funding formulas were such that equalization aid barely made a dent in the vast disparities in school district expenditures.

RODRIGUEZ

The California decision spurred court action across the country. Within little more than a year, six similar court rulings were handed down in Arizona, Kansas, Michigan, Minnesota, New Jersey and Texas.

The Iowa and Minnesota legislatures enacted major school aid reform measures in 1971, followed a year later by California. Enthusiasm for reform, coupled with state budget surpluses and newly available federal revenue sharing, brought the frenzy for equalization to a peak as the states went into their 1973 legislative sessions.

But then, on March 21, 1973, the Supreme Court handed down its 5-4 decision in *San Antonio v. Rodriguez*, declining to declare education a fundamental right under the 14th Amendment. However, the Court did not uphold the status quo in school aid. In the majority opinion, Justice Lewis F. Powell Jr. said, "The need is apparent for reform in tax systems. And certainly innovative new thinking as to public education, its methods and its funding, is necessary." However, reform was not for the Court to achieve. "The ultimate solutions must come from the lawmakers and from the democratic pressures of those who elect them."

Surprisingly, the negative response of the Supreme Court did not significantly hinder the reform movement. Less than two weeks after the *Rodriguez* decision, the New Jersey Supreme Court invalidated that state's system on state constitutional grounds. Ten states enacted school aid reforms in 1973, an all-time high, and an 11th state, Oregon, passed a reform measure that was overturned by the voters in a referendum.

ECONOMY

The recession did not stop the reform movement, either. Two state legislatures enacted school aid reforms in 1974, four in 1975, and one so far this year.

Court activity also continues, although set back in 1975 when two state supreme courts (Idaho and Washington) upheld the school finance systems in their states. Lower courts in two other states, Kansas and Connecticut, overturned their state systems. Suits currently are pending in about a dozen states.

FUNDAMENTAL QUESTION

The most fundamental question of school finance has yet to be resolved—does money make a difference in Johnny's ability to read? School reformers contend that this is a side issue, that the central issue is the right of every child to equal access to equal education.

David C. Long of the Washington-based Lawyers' Committee for Civil Rights Under Law, said, "The notion that a child's education should depend on property wealth has been totally undermined in the last five years. Gradually, the disparities are being chipped away. They can't justify the disparities anymore."

However, F. John Shannon, assistant director of the Advisory Commission on Intergovernmental Relations, cautioned that "conservative legislators are going to use this argument (questioning the effectiveness of school expenditures) for ammunition. In a time of tight money, it won't help the reform movement."

GREATER EQUITY

The most straightforward way to achieve school funding, many reformers once thought, was for the states to take over the job of paying for public education. But state takeovers have proven to be the least acceptable approach.

In general, most state equalization plans try to make up the difference between what the richest districts in the state can afford and what the poorest districts can raise. As yet, few achieve this goal. Because the disparities are so enormous in many states, some laws place ceilings on how much a locality can raise. A few have enacted provisions to "recapture" the excess from rich districts and give it to poor districts. These acts have also been nicknamed "Robin Hood" laws.

STATE TAKEOVER

Only one state—Hawaii—actually assumes total responsibility for financing public elementary and secondary education. In 1969 and 1973, the Advisory Commission on Intergovernmental Relations urged states gradually to take over that function. In 1972, the President's Commission on School Finance came to the same conclusion.

"We're making very slow progress on takeover, but much greater progress on equalization," said Shannon of the intergovernmental relations commission. "Takeover raises concern about the local control issue. People fear that if the state assumes financing, they will lose control of education at the local level. It is a highly emotional issue. In addition, we've found some economic problems with takeover."

One reason for the commission's recommendation for takeover, he explained, was to enable municipalities to use the education portion of the property tax for other purposes. But to get the bills passed, the states have to offer substantial property tax relief, Shannon said. "This leads to enormous windfall profits, particularly for some businesses." What appeared to be the simplest solution breeds its own complexities.

Although no states have taken over school financing completely, nearly every reform state has increased its share of the cost of public schools. The Legislators' Education Action Project computed the increase in 18 states after one year and found that, on the average, state expenditures went up from 39 percent to 51 percent. However, figures for all states show that between the 1969–70 and 1975–76 school years, the federal, state and local shares of education expenditures varied only minimally, while overall expenditures for public education went up by 65 percent.

MAINE

The 1975 Maine school finance law was an attempt to distribute funds for education almost as if school finance were a state program, although half the money was raised at the local level.

"The philosophy as expressed in the act is to create a local-state partnership in the financing of public school education—50 percent of the costs of education to be raised through a uniform local property tax and the remaining 50 percent to be raised from state revenue sources," explained Maine deputy education commissioner Asa A. Gordon in a 1975 paper. "In simple language, money is collected by taxing property wherever it is, and together with state dollars, money is distributed to educate children wherever they are."

The formula to achieve this equalization is enormously complex. Basically, the school costs per pupil are determined for each school district each year. A uniform property tax rate is assessed and levied by each municipality. The municipality sends the state its property tax revenue in monthly installments. The state sends back a school allocation, based on the per-pupil costs of each district. Rich districts don't get back as much as they send in; poor districts get back more. For instance, under this "Robin Hood" recapture provision, the wealthy district of Acton paid into the state $132,000 more than it got back.

Localities were permitted to raise some additional education support. If a district could raise $125 per child with a 2.5 mill levy, it could keep the money for enrichment. But if a 1 mill levy raised less than $50 per pupil, the state would add enough to bring it up to $50.

Education reformers around the country hailed the Maine act. Rich Maine communities were furious with it and, in fact, filed suit against it. A concerted effort was made in the 1976 legislative session to overturn the recapture provision, but it remained in the act, although many other provisions were diluted.

State Sen. Bennett D. Katz, R, a proponent of the Maine reform act, said, "We were able to maintain all the basic ingredients of the act, although we actually made some significant compromises. The reason? We don't have any money. We are in a position of declining revenues." In order to maintain equalization, the legislature agreed to have the state pick up $18 million in local school costs, transferring the burden from the local property tax to the state income tax. "The governor feels that education is guilty of wild spending. He vetoed it. We overrode it by one vote," Katz said.

EQUALIZATION

Equalization formulas take many different forms in different states. In Minnesota, for example, each district levies a 30 mill rate and the state makes up the difference between the amount raised and the state average. Strict levy limits have been imposed. A locality is permitted to exceed the limit by referendum—but no referendum for this purpose ever has passed.

In Texas—the location of the *Rodriguez* case—the poorest district had been able to spend only $400 per child compared with $7,300 in the richest district. In 1975, the legislature enacted an equalizing formula and overhauled property tax assessments.

"Although it is a good provision, this legislation must be classified as foot-in-the-door legislation. They made so many school districts eligible that, with the amount appropriated, the aid equaled only $23 per kid," explained Jose Cardenas, now the executive director of the Intercultural Development Research Association. He was the superintendent of the San Antonio school district that formed the basis of the *Rodriguez* case.

CONTROLS

Many of the reform states have local expenditure controls or ceilings to discourage rich localities from adopting school spending measures out of proportion to state wealth. The New Mexico law permits no exceptions; others permit them in special circumstances.

Wisconsin adopted a Robin Hood recapture measure in its 1973 school aid reform, but delayed implementation until the 1976–77 school year. This year, less than 20 rich districts were scheduled to pay in $3.1 million to be redistributed to more than 400 poorer districts. Gov. Patrick J. Lucey was very anxious to implement the measure, but the legislature wants to delay the payments for another year.

Robert Lang of the Wisconsin legislature's fiscal bureau explained, "This is a key year. First of all, it is the first year of payments. More important, however, is the potential for the future. Each year more and more districts are scheduled to pay. There will be a greater negative impact each year."

The provision, called "negative aids" in Wisconsin, passed in 1973 because it was only one measure in a large package of "must" legislation, the state was flush with a surplus and it was impossible to predict two years down the line whether a district would gain or lose under the recapture clause, Lang said.

Lucey urged implementation of the negative aids provision, but the State Senate voted for delay by a 24 to 8 margin and the Assembly, by a 58 to 37 vote. The governor vetoed the bill; the Senate overrode the veto. The legislature adjourned before the Assembly could act, but it returns in June for a three-day veto session. The prognosis is not bright.

URBAN DIMENSION

"Property wealth once was a good measure of a county's ability to raise money. But cities still look rich on most property-wealth measures," said Berke of the Educational Testing Service. Therefore, more sophisticated measures of wealth must be developed, he said.

Allan Odden, director of the Education Finance Center of the Denver-based Education Commission of the States, explained in an interview that "different measures of wealth affect different kinds of school districts differently: whether you measure property wealth per pupil or per capita, for instance, or how you look at personal income. We are encouraging states to look at all the measures, to analyze them, and to develop a rationale for wealth that fits the state."

The National Urban Coalition studied more sophisticated measures of need, including population density, extraordinary tax rates, the price differential for education services, concentrations of hard-to-educate pupils, and other fiscal problems beyond the control of the local district.

"Urban school finance dollars do not buy the same education resources as the dollars of rural areas and suburban areas," it reported in a paper on geographic adjustments to school aid formulas.

Cities have high concentrations of low-achieving pupils. They must pay higher salaries to teachers. And they must spend a greater portion of their total budgets on noneducational services.

Robert O. Bothwell of the National Urban Coalition, principal author of the paper, explained: "We looked at the fiscal impact in 10 major reform states. From solely a property-wealth standpoint, the reforms clearly have been a boon. Two-thirds of 47 cities are getting greater state aid per pupil. But, when you measure need in more complex ways, only 44 percent of the needy urban areas really benefited" under the reforms.

BROADER MEASURES

A few of the early reforms included a broader measure of wealth than just property tax revenues. In the late 1960s, for example, Rhode Island included personal income as a part of its school aid formula. The 1971 Minnesota reform gave extra weight in its formula to children from families receiving welfare payments in the Aid to Families with Dependent Children category.

For the most part, however, the broader measures are a new phenomenon. Berke sees it as a result of federal poverty aid of the 1960s which expanded the notion of how to measure poverty.

The Connecticut legislature, in 1975, devised a formula that measures assessed property valuation per capita as modified by median family income. The per capita measure takes into account the high percentage of elderly and single people in central cities. One advantage the Connecticut legislature had, according to Odden of the education commission, was the availability of computer simulations that showed how each proposed formula would affect each area of the state.

Another innovation made by some states is to base aid payments on "average daily membership" of classes rather than the traditional "average daily attendance." This accommodates areas with high absentee rates.

Suit

The four largest cities in New York are testing in the courts the concept of broader measurements for urban areas. On April 21, the State Supreme Court began hearing a case brought by New York City, Buffalo, Rochester and Syracuse. The four cities contend that the state aid formula does not take the special needs of large cities into account.

New York City deputy school chancellor Bernard R. Gifford, who developed much of the data for the suit, charged that the formula "does not consider the inordinately high public service expenditures—health care, welfare, mass transportation, public safety, as well as education—that urban districts must and do sustain." He further maintained that the formula "fails to take into account the extra expense of educating the large number of disadvantaged and handicapped children in the cities."

THE "ARMY"

Observers of school finance reform credit much of the success of the "revolution" in education finance to the "army" attracted to the cause.

"The old-timers were old school superintendents who had become school aid technicians. Their perspective was narrow. There is a new gang on the scene that understands the technical aspects, but also knows intergovernmental aid and law. This means more legislation, more practical proposals," according to Kelly of the Ford Foundation.

Berke agreed: "The kind of people involved (in school aid reform) changed in the 1960s. Many have a legal background. The field has busted open with a new opportunity to rethink a lot of the old concepts."

The "foot soldiers" in the revolution include the Lawyers' Committee for Civil Rights Under Law and other legal groups involved in the court cases as well as activist governors and state legislators who have written and guided the reforms through state assemblies.

A wide array of citizens' groups and other organizations have provided essential support services, conducting the studies that develop the formulas and mobilizing public support through "education" campaigns.

ORGANIZATIONS

On the national level, the Education Fund of the League of Women Voters of the U.S., the Education Commission of the States, the Legislators' Education Action Project of the National Conference of State Legislatures and the National Urban Coalition are among the main groups that provide the support and "educational" services, often with Ford Foundation support.

The National Education Association monitors the progress of education finance reform and has intervened in some state court cases.

State and local groups either separately or in coalitions with the national organizations usually provide the local base for action. For example, the Citizens League, a powerful civic group in the seven-county Twin Cities metropolitan area of Minnesota, developed the reform bill in that state in 1970. The successful gubernatorial candidate—Wendell R. Anderson—made it a part of his campaign that fall. The act was passed with few significant changes.

SOUTH CAROLINA

The League of Women Voters Education Fund has had a Ford Foundation grant for three years to work on school aid reform in New Jersey, South Carolina and Vermont. Currently, they are concentrating on South Carolina, where a bill was introduced in the legislature in March.

South Carolina distributes education aid through flat grants to school districts. The amounts vary little from rich to poor districts. The league—working with a local group called the Citizens Coalition for S.C. School Financing—developed various options for equalizing the aid program. A bill combining several of these ideas was introduced in the legislature. Now the league—again through the coalition —is pushing that bill.

MISSOURI

Although the participants deny that school aid reform is a national movement or that they form a network, the reformers maintain close contact and comprise an informal "school aid fraternity."

The efforts of several of these groups will converge in Missouri in December for the Governor's Conference on Education. Historically, when the Missouri governor calls a major conference on a subject, orders studies and obtains widespread support, the proposals developed at the conference are enacted, according to the education commission's Odden.

Missouri has a basic foundation program, authorized to provide $400 per school child across the state. According to Odden, the state actually provides $600 per child, but the formula still needs to be equalized.

The Education Commission of the States is studying the financial aspects of the program. "We're analyzing the results of the current system, how great are the disparities," Odden said. "We're going to develop alternative policy options. Also, we are looking at the tax structure. Who pays the taxes? Where is the revenue raised? We are all very optimistic that something will come out of this conference—because of the history of success."

FEDERAL ROLE

Historically, the federal government has played a neutral role in school finance reform, although substantial amounts of federal aid have been targeted to poor children.

FEDERAL AID

President Johnson's war on poverty doubled the federal share of public education support in the two years between 1965 and 1967. But the federal portion of the total public school spending dollar remained small, increasing from 4.3 to 8.8 percent. The major vehicle of this increase was the Elementary and Secondary Education Act of 1965 (79 Stat 27). Title I provided categorical aid for disadvantaged school children, primarily in the inner cities.

"Because it is based primarily on personal income and goes to areas of substantial disadvantage, Title I has introduced an element of equalization," Berke said. "However, federal aid has not amounted to a great percentage of the gross, and most federal aid has come in the form of categorical programs that don't equalize at all. However, I think you could say that Title I and other federal poverty programs have shown the way for equalization by developing broadened measurements of poverty."

Callahan of the legislators' conference has a different view. In the introduction of a recent conference report, *School Finance Reform: A Legislators' Handbook* (NCSL, 1976), he wrote: "Efforts to make state school finance legislation more equitable in the near future are likely to be hampered not only by shortfalls in the state tax collections but also by the failure of the federal government to provide appropriate support for state reform efforts. . . .

"Thus far, only the federal government's continued funding of the Title I compensatory education program and its recent creation of small-scale educational block grants have proved of major assistance to state finance reform efforts."

Callahan singled out the federal impact aid program—the so-called PL 874 program—as particularly disequalizing. Instituted in 1950, the intention of the program is to compensate areas "impacted" by federal installations that send children to the public schools but do not pay the local property taxes to support them.

Over the years, several Presidents have tried to modify or cut back impact aid, but affected Members of Congress are loathe to let their districts lose the money, and impact aid always is kept.

The 1974 Education Amendments (88 Stat 484) for the first time tried to mitigate the disequalizing effect of impact aid by permitting reform states to consider impact aid as state aid in their equalization formulas. Some four states are eligible under this provision, which is just going into effect after a long process of developing guidelines.

Equalization Grants

The 1974 amendments also took the first federal step toward subsidizing state equalization. Very quietly, with little publicity, the Senate tucked into the measure a provision (Section 842) for such aid.

The Administration did not ask for the provision, has not sought funding for it and—now that the regulations have been published—is not publicizing the availability of the aid, which would provide grants ranging from $100,000 for Alaska to $1 million for California for states to develop or implement equalization plans. Federal officials indicate that "general conformity" with the guidelines is all that is required to participate in the program.

Some 30 states are expected to apply for funds under Section 842 even in the absence of any federal publicity about the program.

ADMINISTRATION POSITIONS

In the past four years, the Administration has not taken a stand on school finance reform.

In March 1970, President Nixon established the President's Commission on School Finance to study the federal government's role. By early 1972, it was ready to report and recommend that the states assume the responsibility for financial reform, with the federal role remaining indirect and minimal.

Two months before the commission issued its report, Nixon, in his State of the Union message, proposed a comprehensive federal program of federal aid to states to equalize education and provide property tax relief. It would be funded by a federal value-added tax.

Nixon asked the Advisory Commission on Intergovernmental Relations to study the proposal. The commission's report to the President, issued in January 1973, gave its answer in the title: "Financing Schools and Property Tax Relief—A State Responsibility." Not only the commission opposed the idea; in the intervening year, public opinion had turned against the proposal as well. It was withdrawn quietly.

NEA PROPOSAL

The National Education Association has continued to support a major increase in federal support for public education. It seeks an amendment to general revenue sharing to permit counties to use their allotment for education support. At present, only states can support education from general revenue sharing funds.

In addition, the education association has proposed raising the federal share of education spending to one-third of the total.

In a statement adopted last Oct. 9, the association called on "the federal government (to) make a bold commitment to improve the quality and equality of education by guaranteeing a national standard of quality education for all public schools and broadening the base for school support in order to equalize education opportunity for all children."

House Education and Labor Committee chairman Carl D. Perkins, D-Ky., introduced the measure in the House (HR 10145); Sen. Claiborne Pell, D-R.I., sponsored a companion bill in the Senate. However, no hearings have been held and no action is likely this year.

LEGISLATORS

Callahan of the state legislatures' conference summed up his organization's position on federal aid:

"Over the long haul, all that the conference is asking is for Congress and the Administration to be reasonable about education funding levels and to develop a funding system that builds on the advances that the states exhibit."

OUTLOOK

"Ten years ago," said the Ford Foundation's Kelly, "not 10 people were interested in school aid reform. Six years ago, not a single judge had held a day's hearings on the subject—not a single legislature had acted. Then, in the intervening five years, suddenly there was the availability of general revenue sharing funds and relatively inflation-proof increases in state revenue resources. And a good number of states made significant changes.

"But then, in the last two years, three things occurred: first, the states in which reform was easy moved; second, the level of inflation rose; and third, the states have suffered cyclical budgetary declines. Therefore, there has been little movement recently. But beneath the surface, a lot is simmering. We'll see some more activity in the next couple of years."

Odden, of the Education Commission of the States, made a somewhat similar assessment: "I see the situation as kind of a trough right now. First of all, the economy is poor. There are just not a lot of excess funds around for the states to enact new reforms. Secondly, it is an election year. States are unlikely to do anything big. However, I think '77 will be a different story. The Missouri study is on the horizon. California is gearing up to act. And New York might act next year. States to watch right now are South Carolina and maybe Tennessee and Louisiana."

The intergovernmental relations commission's Shannon also suggested looking to the South for changes:

"I think many of the new reforms will take place in the South. The economic wind is to the back of the Southern states and the energy-rich states. Reform usually requires money. The only exception is the judicial one. Several school cases are pending and we might have some action in those states, New Jersey in particular."

Summed up Kelly: "The decade of the '70s will be looked back on as the era in which really great reform took place."

8

School Financing
Undergoes a Revolution

Ward Sinclair

IT HAS NOT inspired flashy headlines, but a quiet and unconcluded revolution is radically changing the way the American public pays for its schools.

Motivated by challenges to traditional school support through property taxes, more than 20 states since 1970 have taken steps to make all districts' spending on pupils more nearly equal.

More changes seem likely in other states.

Pending litigation will affect some. And in virtually every state where reform has not occurred, legislatures or commissions are studying the issue, according to the Education Commission of the States.

The changes affect the way the public pays its taxes, how much it pays, the programs that schools offer, the decisions home buyers make when picking a place to live.

Generally, what is occurring is a shift in the school financing burden from the local level to the states, with an accompanying shift away from local property taxes and onto other revenue sources.

Ten years ago, 52.7 percent of school revenues across the country came from local sources, 39.3 percent from the state level and 8.0 percent from the federal level.

The federal share has not changed; it was 8.3 percent in the school year just past. But the local share has fallen to 47.6 percent, while the state share has risen to 44.1 percent, making them almost equal.

In some states, as a corollary, local property taxes have been cut. Reductions have run as high as 10 percent in Colorado, Florida and Wisconsin, to cite three examples.

Maine, Montana and Utah set up guaranteed school support programs, then "recaptured" from their wealthiest districts the locally raised tax money that exceeded guaranteed levels. Hawaii took over the full cost of its public schools.

New Jersey, after losing a lawsuit, was forced to relieve local property tax burdens and revamp its general school support program. The result was adoption of an income tax in 1976 to pay the new state education expenses.

In California, after the state supreme court said in 1971 that the local property tax–based finance system was unconstitutional, more state money was provided to schools and local assessment disparities were eliminated.

Both Maryland and Virginia have taken steps to provide more aid to local schools, but the percentage of their assistance actually has declined during the decade.

According to the National Education Association, Virginia's share fell from 37.3 percent in 1967–68 to 31.8 percent in 1977–78. Maryland's share dipped from 35.8 percent to 34.2 percent.

In Maryland, state aid from general funds was increased $120 million in the last six years. But major disparities persisted from district to district. Affluent Montgomery County in 1976–77 spent $2,119 per pupil—with 73 percent of that raised locally. Cecil County, in contrast, spent $1,256 per pupil, with 42.9 percent from local sources.

Virginia's school-funding controversy has been intense since 1971, when a revised state constitution required the General Assembly to set uniform standards of quality for public education.

The new standards forced many small cities and rural counties to make major increases in local spending, putting new pressure on property taxes. Rural and urban government officials contend the state should pay more to help them meet the state-imposed standards. Urban officials additionally complain that the complicated school money distribution formula, based on local tax capacity, favors rural counties.

"From the educational-equity as well as the tax aspects of it, yes, it is a revolution," said Dick Kohn, a school-finance attorney at the Lawyers Committee for Civil Rights Under Law.

The basis for it is relatively simple: tax practices and property wealth, which vary from district to district, are seen as tools that perpetrate unequal spending on education within a state.

And courts are holding that state constitutions, which generally assure equal educational opportunity for all pupils, are violated by traditional financing practices.

The newest court ruling, and potentially one of the most influential, came two weeks ago in New York. That case added another dimension—that kids in big cities are entitled to special school aid.

The New York ruling is the latest in a series. Other notables include California, where the landmark decision came in 1971, New Jersey and Connecticut. They have helped set the pace for change.

The lawyers committee, funded largely by the Ford Foundation, has been involved in a dozen or more other cases around the country, and is working on litigation in South Dakota, Arkansas, Georgia, West Virginia and Massachusetts.

While the immediate impact in the classroom is more difficult to assess, some points show up in those states where changes have occurred:

• Gaps in per-pupil spending are being closed between the affluent and the property-poor districts, in theory lessening the differences that make one's schools more appealing than another.

• The idea of local control, through which the level of local support determines the quality of programs, may be diminished by greater state involvement in school-financing.

• States' share of school spending during this period of change has climbed from just more than one-third to slightly over one-half. Much of that state-aid increase is underwritten by federal revenue-sharing money, but new taxes and tax structure reform also have ensued.

If there is an irony in these state-by-state changes, it is that they are not spurred by interpretations of federal law, the engine of major change in public schools during the past 25 years.

Rather, state courts have been taking up where the U.S. Supreme Court left off in 1973, when it said, in a case from San Antonio, that discrimination in school spending is not covered by the U.S. Constitution.

In the Rodriguez case, as it is known, the Supreme Court said the Constitution guarantees no one an education. But most state constitutions, in one way or another, regard education as a right.

In the recent New York case, the judge went beyond the argument that spending disparities—which he found to be violations of the state's constitutional equal protection guarantees—were related to the wealth of individual districts.

Following that argument, districts with above-average property tax bases tax at lower rates, yet they tend to spend more per pupil than districts with low tax bases which levy higher taxes.

But Judge L. Kingsley Smith also held that the state must come up with a plan that will do more than equalize spending. It must also provide additional help for pupils in large cities, where special programs for the disadvantaged add to costs, yet competition for tax dollars undercuts the schools.

The New York decision, although subject to appeal, is being watched closely by school-finance experts as a possible guide for litigation in large urban centers, particularly in the Northeast and Midwest.

"The battle now has been broadened to include educational need," said Bill Wilken, education specialist at the National Conference of State Legislatures.

One part of the New York case involved several dozen "have-not" districts, headed by Levittown, which argued the now common position that a low property tax base undermined their school programs.

The other part involved the cities of New York, Buffalo, Rochester and Syracuse, which were represented by Elliott C. Lichtman, a Washington attorney.

Lichtman's contention was that the existing state financing formula discriminated against the cities because their tax bases were drained by non-school expenditures—the so-called municipal overburden.

He said the "reality of the cities" was ignored by the formula. The reality includes high cost of municipal services, higher cost of living, the additional expense of teaching disadvantaged pupils, an aid formula that reduced state payments as absenteeism rose.

"The overburden argument is very important, but it won't work in all large cities," said Gus Steinhilber of the National School Boards Association. "If there is litigation along these lines, it will be important in the cities of the Northeast and around the Great Lakes."

Kohn, of the lawyers committee, noted that similar overburden arguments have been litigated in Cincinnati and Seattle. But he said the New Look opinion is "a tremendous breakthrough."

These observers agree that popular demands for property tax reform have run hand in hand with the school finance overhaul drive, each feeding on the other.

An open question is whether and how much the taxpayer sentiment stirred up by the success of California's tax-cutting Proposition 13 will affect school finances.

As Wilken pointed out, "Providing more state aid has been a convenient way of making the property tax more manageable at the local level. Proposition 13 may make it harder to pull this off."

Kohn takes another view. "It is hard to assess the impact, but a Proposition 13–type move may achieve what we are trying to do anyway—eliminate the property tax as a means of school funding."

Whatever, there is still no easy answer to the schools' demands for more money. New York is the classic.

"If New York is upheld, I don't envy the legislature," Wilken said. "The normal solution is to put more money in the pot and give it to the have-nots."

He added, "The state's taxes and its spending on education is way out of line with everyone else, yet you have disparities between districts there. In Kansas or Iowa, for instance, it would be easier to pull off changes than in New York. It will tax everyone's ingenuity."

9

Black Excellence—
The Case of Dunbar High School

Thomas Sowell

SOCIAL PATHOLOGY HAS held an enduring fascination for researchers, and nowhere more so than in the study of black Americans. Isolated "successes" or "heroes" receive occasional attention, but large-scale or institutionalized progress and excellence seem almost to be shunned, except for passing references to the "middle-class" end results. With all the voluminous outpourings on black educational pathology, there has been an almost total neglect of one of the most remarkable black educational success stories: Dunbar High School.

For a period of 85 years (1870–1955) Dunbar was an academically elite, all-black public high school in Washington, D.C. As far back as 1899, Dunbar students came in first in citywide tests given in both black and white schools. Over the 85-year span, most of Dunbar's graduates went on to college, even though most Americans—white or black—did not. Most Dunbar graduates could afford only to attend the low-cost local colleges: either federally-supported Howard University or tuition-free Miner Teachers College. However, those Dunbar graduates who attended Harvard, Amherst, Oberlin, and other prestigious institutions (usually on scholarships) ran up an impressive record of academic honors. For example, it is known that Amherst admitted 34 Dunbar graduates between 1892 and 1954; of these, 74 percent graduated, and more than one-fourth of these graduates were Phi Beta Kappas.

In their careers, as in their academic work, Dunbar graduates excelled. The first black general (Benjamin O. Davis), the first black

91

federal judge (William H. Hastie), the first black Cabinet member (Robert C. Weaver), the discoverer of blood plasma (Charles Drew), and the first black Senator since Reconstruction (Edward W. Brooke) were all Dunbar graduates. During World War II, Dunbar graduates in the Army included "nearly a score of majors, nine colonels and lieutenant colonels, and one brigadier general"[1]—a substantial percentage of the total number of high-ranking black officers at that time.

Almost as astonishing as Dunbar's achievements has been the ignoring of those achievements—which might, after all, conceivably have some bearing on questions about educating black children. No scholarly study of the school has yet appeared, and almost the entire literature on the subject consists of one slim volume, *The Dunbar Story*, printed privately at her own expense by Mary Gibson Hundley, a retired Dunbar teacher. Where Dunbar has been noticed at all, it has been brushed aside as a "middle-class" black school, and local tradition in Washington suggests that its students were predominantly light-skinned Negroes, many scarcely distinguishable from whites. The facts do not support either assertion, but the attempt to dismiss the Dunbar experience is a significant phenomenon in its own right.

HISTORY

What are the facts and factors in the Dunbar story? First of all, Dunbar High School, as it existed from its founding in 1870 to the school reorganization following the Supreme Court's integration decision in 1954, is no more. The name and the building are still there, but it is now just another ghetto school—in appearance, atmosphere and statistical profile. It is more fortunate than most in having a dedicated principal, but she is clearly struggling against the odds. Alumni who refer to "Dunbar when it was Dunbar" do not help her, or today's students, but they are expressing a bitter historical truth.

The unique educational phenomenon that was Dunbar High School occurred between 1870 and 1955. The experience began in a basement school, changed locations and names,[2] but maintained institutional continuity and high academic standards. It was the first black high school in the United States, and it was an academic school from the beginning—fiercely resisting recurrent pressures upon it to become vocational, commercial, or "general." It taught Latin throughout this period, and in some early years Greek as well. It was never "relevant" to the passing fads, but it instilled individual and racial pride. In the building it has occupied since 1916, the auditorium is dominated by a verse by black poet Paul Laurence Dunbar:

> Keep a-pluggin' away,
> Perseverance still is king . . .

Why this particular school—and why Washington, D.C.? There is no ready answer. Certainly there was nothing radically distinctive about the Washington black community through most of the 20th century, and since Dunbar was unique from the outset, the elements of that uniqueness are probably best found in history and in the traditions generated by its early success.

Back in 1870, the Washington black community was in fact unique. Although slavery had ended just five years earlier, the Washington Negro community was much older than that. As far back as 1830, half the Negroes in Washington were free. Before the Civil War started, 78 percent of the blacks in Washington were free. As the slave states of the South progressively tightened up their restrictions on the "free persons of color" in the decades preceding the Civil War, Washington became something of a Mecca for those free Negroes seeking a better life. The federal government's presence made Washington less oppressive than the Southern slave states and also opened employment opportunities in government jobs better than those open to black people elsewhere.

The Washington black community was thus more than a generation ahead in freedom and acculturation. Moreover, Dunbar was not a neighborhood school, but drew upon the entire black community of Washington for its students. It was in a similarly favorable position in recruiting its teachers and principals. Given the extreme scarcity of educated Negroes in 1870, Dunbar's performance could not be readily duplicated elsewhere within any reasonable span of years. The first black woman to receive a college degree in the United States graduated from Oberlin in 1862—and taught at Dunbar. The first black man to graduate from Harvard received his degree in 1870 and became principal of Dunbar in 1872. For decades to come, Dunbar would have its choice of teachers with outstanding academic credentials. Four of its first eight principals graduated from Oberlin and two from Harvard. Some had graduate degrees as well. Dunbar had three Ph.D.'s on its teaching staff in the 1920's, due to the almost total exclusion of blacks from most college and university faculties.

(It was 1942 before there was a black senior faculty member at any major university—and he was a Dunbar graduate.)

In short, as the first black high school, Dunbar had its pick of potential teachers and principals. By its early reputation for excellence, it continued to attract them. Segregation and discrimination gave a captive market of both students and teachers. But though these may have been necessary conditions for Dunbar's success, they were hardly sufficient. What Washington also had was a black community that demanded academic excellence even in 1870, and continued to fight tenaciously for it over the years. As early as 1807, the approximately 500 "free persons of color" in the District of Columbia built a small school house for their children. Over the next several decades they sent their children to private schools before they were allowed in the public schools. When the "colored trustees" of the D.C. public school system established the first high school in 1870, they were planting it in fertile ground.

THE FOUNDERS

The achievements of Dunbar no doubt also reflect the personal qualities of individual leaders during the institution's formative years. A special kind of confidence and courage must have been required for a black man or woman to pioneer at Oberlin or Harvard in the middle of the 19th century, when the very capacity of the race for education was openly questioned, even by liberals opposed to slavery. The early Dunbar principals had to be individuals not easily discouraged, frightened, or inclined to compromise about quality. This is how historical accounts describe them. Certainly this became the dominant tradition of the school.

The head of the group which founded the first high school for Negroes was a remarkable man named William Syphax. He grew up as a free man, having been freed in infancy in 1826, and became a civil rights activist in the Washington Negro community in the mid-19th century. He was described as a man of "dauntless courage and unwavering integrity" who "dared to demand what was due his race, fearing no man regardless of position or color." The substance and tone of his messages to municipal and federal officials clearly support this description. He was hard-headed on education. While the group he led preferred Negro teachers for Negro children—other things being equal—they were not prepared to compromise quality for the sake of racial representation, for they deemed it a "violation of our official oath to employ inferior teachers when superior teachers can be had for the same money." Syphax was equally frank in telling the black community that it would have to send its children to school with respect for teachers and a willingness to submit to discipline and hard work, if their education was to amount to anything.[3]

The early principals were equally remarkable people. Mary Jane Patterson not only was the first black woman in the United States to earn a college degree, she did it by spurning the usual courses for women at Oberlin, and taking instead a program of Greek, Latin, and higher mathematics designed for "gentlemen." As principal, she was "a strong, forceful personality," noted for "thoroughness," and for being "an indefatigable worker." She was principal for a dozen years in the formative period of the school.[4]

A successor as principal, Robert H. Terrell, "devoted most of his time out of school to preparing boys for college," with the result that "a goodly number" later "completed their education at Harvard"[5]— and this at the turn of the century. The tradition continued as the school changed principals and buildings. In the period 1918–1923, Dunbar graduates earned 15 degrees from Ivy League colleges and universities, and 10 degrees from Amherst, Williams, and Wesleyan.

Throughout the period of its academic ascendancy, Dunbar was characterized by the esprit of its students, the dedication of its teachers, and the strong support of the community, both in everyday chores and in episodic crises. Special efforts were made to get college scholarships for bright but poor youngsters. Indeed, special efforts were often needed to get the parents of such youngsters to keep them in high school, instead of sending them to work to bring home some much-needed help for family finances. One concrete indicator of student attitude is the record of attendance and tardiness. A spot check of old Board of Education records in both categories shows Dunbar's record to have been superior to the average of its white counterparts, both around the turn of the century (1901–1902) and around mid-century (1952–1953).

DUNBAR I.Q.'s

The argument has often been made that I.Q.'s have little relationship to performance as far as black people are concerned; however, there is already a considerable literature indicating that I.Q. and similar tests are equally accurate predictors of black and white academic performance. Dunbar provides a somewhat different kind of test of this hypothesis, based on a black group with outstanding performances in both academic and career terms. Are Dunbar I.Q.'s significantly different from the national average I.Q. of 85 for black Americans? The table below answers that question:

MEAN I.Q. OF DUNBAR STUDENTS

Class of	All Students	Graduates Only	Non-Graduates Only
1938	105.5	111.6	97.1
1939	111.2	114.0	101.9
1940	108.5	111.1	100.9
1941	109.3	111.7	101.7
1942	105.2	107.8	101.4
1943	101.3	102.6	98.5
1944	106.0	109.8	97.5
1945	98.8	101.6	93.5
1946	102.1	105.7	102.1
1947	102.6	108.4	94.9
1948	105.3	106.5	98.2
1949	106.1	106.1	104.0
1950	110.9	111.3	99.4
1951	102.7	103.4	98.1
1952	103.1	104.7	94.3
1953	101.3	102.7	93.5
1954	101.7	102.6	98.8
1955	99.6	100.8	96.4

Dunbar students' average I.Q.'s were substantially higher than those of other blacks as reported in numerous surveys, and usually were above the national average as well. Even the Dunbar dropouts scored higher than the average of other blacks. It should be noted that Dunbar students were not selected on the basis of I.Q. tests. Indeed, admission to Dunbar was a matter of individual self-selection. No one was automatically assigned to Dunbar, because it was not a neighborhood school during the 1870–1955 period. Nor was it likely that anyone merely happened to enroll there, since its reputation and standards were well-known throughout the local black community. Indeed, some black youngsters from nearby Maryland and Virginia were known to give false D.C. addresses in order to attend.

The high I.Q.'s at Dunbar were hardly the whole story, however.

An equal number of black students scattered elsewhere with equal I.Q.'s might not have produced an equal number of high academic and career performances, because certain other factors would have been lacking: (1) the motivational element associated with self-selection for such a school; (2) the benefits of mutual association with high-quality students and with teachers attracted to teaching such students; and (3) the school traditions, including distinguished alumni who were constantly being held up as examples to the students. Certainly, the kind of personal interest, counseling, and extra-curricular tutoring which Dunbar students received is extremely rare for black students today, whether in all-black or in integrated schools. A recent Ford Foundation study, for example, has reported the quality of counseling available to black students to be "markedly inadequate" in both North and South, and the testimony of college recruiters paints an even grimmer picture of neglect or distorted "guidance" given to black students.[6]

Clearly not essential to the Dunbar performance was racial integration, outstanding physical facilities, or generous financial support. It had none of these. Except for a few white teachers in its early days in the 1870's, Dunbar was an all-Negro school, from students to teachers to administrators, for generation after generation. Moreover, it was located in a segregated city, where as recently as 1950 Negroes were not admitted to most downtown movie theaters or restaurants. The physical facilities of Dunbar were always inadequate; its lunchroom was so small that many students had to eat lunch out on the street, and it was 1950 before the school had a public address system. Dunbar was part of a segregated school system, administered by whites at the top and perennially starved for funds. Internally, there were class-conscious and color-conscious cliques among students, and resentment of administration favoritism among the teachers. In short, the list of "prerequisites" for success in which educators indulge themselves was clearly not met at Dunbar.

I.Q.'s AND SEX

There is evidence that Dunbar was at its peak some time before the period when I.Q. scores were recorded. The slight downward drift of I.Q.'s over the 1938–1955 period is in keeping with the impression that this was the declining phase of its academic prime. The 1938–1955 period was studied statistically because this is the only period during Dunbar's academic prime for which I.Q. scores are available. Over the 18-year span, girls outnumbered boys every year—usually by about two to one, but by as much as three to one in the class of 1952. This conforms to a general predominance of females among high I.Q. American Negroes—a baffling phenomenon, difficult to explain by either hereditary or environmental theories or by the cultural bias of the tests. Black males and females obviously draw upon the same pool of genes. They are also raised in the same environment. True, this environment creates sex role differentiation, but I.Q. tests are so structured as to produce virtually identical averages for males and females in the general population. Nevertheless, higher female I.Q.'s remain a persistent phenomenon among American Negroes, even though different tests are used in different times and places. I.Q. results from an all-male and an all-female junior high school (J.H.S. 139 and J.H.S. 136, respectively) serving the same neighborhood in central Harlem for a 20-year period (1941–1960) show the female school to have had a higher average I.Q. for all but one of the years for which such data were available. The particular I.Q. test used varied, but the relative standings of the sexes were virtually constant.

The higher I.Q.'s of black females might be cultural peculiarity (along the lines of the Moynihan thesis, for example) or they could be a clue to the lower black I.Q. in general. Among human beings as a whole, and even among other mammals, males vary more (physically, emotionally, and mentally) with the environment than do females. If the generally low I.Q. scores of black Americans (or any other group) are due to environment rather than to heredity, it should also be expected that the lower average I.Q. would be accompanied by a degree of sex difference in I.Q. not found in the general population. This is almost invariably the case in studies of black American I.Q.'s. It is also true of studies of working class I.Q.'s in Britain, so it is hardly a racial characteristic.

CLASS AND COLOR

Given the general predominance of mulattoes among the "free persons of color" and their descendants, it seems probable that the light-skinned mulatto stereotype was applicable to the early Dunbar students and teachers. This group continued for many years to be over-represented among Dunbar students and teachers—but this is not to say that it constituted a majority. A study of old yearbook photographs at Dunbar High School shows the great bulk of the students to have been very much the color of most American Negroes. Any bias in the photography of that period—before black was beautiful—would be toward printing the pictures lighter than life. My impression from visiting a Dunbar reunion also accords with the conclusion that most Dunbar students were not unusually light in complexion.

A study of class records for the period 1938–1955 also confirms that most Dunbar students' parents were not middle-class professionals. Among those students whose parents' occupations could be identified and categorized, the largest single category was consistently "unskilled and semi-skilled," and the median job index was at about the level of a white-collar worker. Perhaps more significantly, the differences in mean I.Q. were relatively slight between students whose parents fell in different occupational categories. For the classes of 1938–1955, the mean I.Q. of students whose parents were in the "unskilled and semi-skilled" category ranged from 96.1 in 1945 to 113.3 in 1950. The mean I.Q. of students whose parents were "professionals" ranged from 102.1 in 1942 to 124.2 in 1950. Moreover, even the academic exclusiveness of Dunbar should not be overstated. Figures available for the period 1938–1948 show that approximately one third of all black students enrolled in D.C. high schools were enrolled in Dunbar.

Although the local stereotype of Dunbar was that it was where the doctors' and lawyers' children went to school (as it probably was), the percentage of Dunbar students whose parents' occupations could be identified as "professional" never exceeded six percent for any of the 18 years surveyed. Since only about half of the parental occupations were identifiable and categorized, this should be regarded as a high of about 12 percent of the occupations known and classified— exceptionally large for a black school, but still a long way from predominance. Former Dunbar principal Charles S. Lofton refers to the middle-class stereotype as "an old wives' tale." "If we took only the children of doctors and lawyers," he asked, "how could we have had 1400 black students at one time?" Similarly, former Dunbar teacher Mary Gibson Hundley wrote: "A large segment of the students had one or more government employees for support. Before the 1940's these employees were messengers and clerks, with few exceptions."[7]

TIME AND TRADITION

It is true, however, that the history and traditions of the school were to a large extent shaped by members of a few prominent families in Washington's Negro community. These were, typically, descendants of the antebellum "free persons of color," light-skinned in general, and in particular cases physically indistinguishable from whites. This group was not numerically dominant, and did not intermarry with the mass of blacks during most of the period under discussion, so it had little biological effect on the rest of the Negro population. (In fact, this small group of families married among themselves to such an extent that it became noted for birth defects.) But it did have a major and enduring cultural impact on the Dunbar community. For example, as late as the 1950's there was a dedicated Dunbar teacher of many years' service who had herself graduated from Dunbar, whose mother had graduated in the class of 1885, and whose grandfather had headed the group that set up the original school in the basement of a church in 1870. She is still active in alumni affairs today.

The history of Dunbar High School places in sharp relief the importance of time and tradition. Not only did the institution have a decisive head start as the first black high school in the country; the community from which it came had a similarly decisive head start in freedom, combined with stable employment opportunities in the federal government, even before the Civil War. These circumstances in turn drew into Washington a nucleus of like-minded and highly qualified Negroes, as well as a larger mass of less favored but also ambitious blacks receptive to their leadership. The individuals who founded and shaped the early history of the institution which became known as Dunbar High School were remarkable people, as is evidenced by their achievements as well as by accounts and descriptions of them. They were not narrow education careerists. Most went on to achieve distinction in other fields—as lawyers, judges, and, in one case, U.S. Consul in Vladivostok. The children and grandchildren of these individuals also went to Dunbar and often became teachers there as well, bringing a tradition and dedication that could not be bought on the open market.

A 20th-reunion survey of the class of 1940 indicates that Dunbar graduates apparently shared a striking characteristic of the black elite:

fertility rates too low even to replace themselves. The married members of the class of 1940 averaged 1.6 children. This is typical of middle-class Negroes: They not only have far fewer children than lower-class Negroes, they have fewer children than whites of the same income or education as themselves. This demographic peculiarity means that a great part of the struggle from poverty to middle-class status has to be repeated in the next generation, for very few black children are born to parents who could start them off with the benefits won by their own struggle.

DECLINE AND FALL

The Supreme Court desegregation decision of 1954 set in motion a series of events which in a few years destroyed all that had been built up over several decades at Dunbar High School. The whole dual school system in Washington had to be reorganized. In this reorganization, all D.C. schools became neighborhood schools. The neighborhood in which Dunbar was located was one of the poorest multiproblem areas of the Washington ghetto. For years it had been the pattern that most youngsters who lived near Dunbar did not go to Dunbar. Now suddenly, they did—and the character of the school began to change drastically. As an interim measure, existing Dunbar students were allowed to continue in school until graduation, regardless of where they lived, and most elected to do so. This postponed the inevitable, but not for long.

Teachers used to bright, eager students began to find learning problems and then disciplinary problems in their classrooms. Advanced courses in mathematics faced dwindling enrollments which finally forced their cancellation, while remedial math courses appeared for the first time. Similar trends were apparent in other subjects as well. The Dunbar teaching staff at that time was somewhat advanced in years, and many began retiring—some as early as the minimum age of 55, whereas in the past it had been common for Dunbar teachers to stay on until the mandatory retirement age of 70. Equally qualified replacements were hard to find, with Dunbar now rapidly becoming a typical ghetto school. Ironically, the drastic changes forced upon Dunbar in the reorganization that followed the 1954 Supreme Court decision had virtually no desegregation effect, given the virtually all-black neighborhood in which the school was located.

Today, the present principal of Dunbar, Mrs. Phyllis Beckwith, spends much of her time dealing with discipline problems: roaming the halls to maintain order, receiving police reports on truants loitering on the streets during school hours, and otherwise struggling to achieve the kind of learning atmosphere earlier Dunbar principals could take for granted. In addition, Mrs. Beckwith spends a considerable amount of her own after-school time maintaining contacts with the still active Dunbar alumni groups—attending class reunions and trying to elicit concern from the old Dunbar graduates for today's very different students. Her dedication is virtually the only reminder today of the Dunbar tradition. To an observer, her efforts seem heroic but largely unappreciated—either by the current students or by the old alumni, who show little sympathy for the students who to them represent the destruction of their school.

The Supreme Court's desegregation decision, as such, did not doom Dunbar High School. Theoretically, Dunbar could have remained an academically elite high school, not tied to neighborhood boundaries, and could have simply opened up to students with regard to race. There have been public schools of this sort in New York, Boston, and other cities. But in the emotionally charged atmosphere of the time, under the strong legal and political pressures to "do something" in the nation's capital, such a resolution was never a realistic possibility. "Neighborhood schools" was the rallying cry of whites resisting total desegregation; "integration" was the battle cry of black leaders. The maintenance of educational quality at a black elite high school had no such emotional appeal or political clout. The school reorganization plan gave something to both sides—a measure of integration and the maintenance of neighborhood schools—and so was a political success. For Dunbar, however, it was an educational catastrophe.

The Board of Education which promulgated the reorganization plan of 1954 that destroyed Dunbar High School seems to have had no appreciation of or concern about this possibility. In the lengthy and bitter debates recorded in the Board of Education minutes, almost every conceivable problem was argued, other than the effect of the reorganization on Dunbar High School. This is all the more remarkable because the Board's most vocal critic of the school superintendent's plan was a Dunbar alumna. Yet even today she cannot recall saying a word about Dunbar High School at the time, even in executive sessions not reported in Board minutes. Integration was the cry of the hour and the fight of the hour.

THE CONDITIONS OF ACHIEVEMENT

Although Dunbar High School was the product of unique historical circumstances, its educational and social achievements have continuing relevance. First of all, it showed what could be done with black children, including substantial numbers from low-income backgrounds. The question of how it was done needs more exploration. It was not done by teaching ethnocentric "relevance," nor was it achieved with generous financing or even with adequate plant and equipment.

What Dunbar had was a solid nucleus of parents, teachers, and principals who knew just what kind of education they wanted and how to produce it. They came from one of the oldest and largest urban black middle classes in the nation. But the beneficiaries of this situation were not exclusively, or even predominantly, middle-class students. Because the knowledge and educational values of the black elite were institutionalized and traditionalized, they became available to generations of low-income black students. Despite the fashionable (and sometimes justified) criticism of the old "black bourgeoisie," they were a source of know-how, discipline, and organization otherwise virtually unavailable to lower-class blacks. The possibilities of transmitting this sophistication from a fortunate segment of the race to a wider range of receptive individuals may now have declined with the exit of the black middle class to the suburbs and with the rise of ideological barriers insulating "militant" black youth from such influences.

The I.Q. scores of Dunbar students averaged very much higher than those of black students in general, indicating that I.Q.'s and achievement are correlated among blacks as among whites. Note that "achievement" here means the subsequent accomplishments of students, rather than the socioeconomic background of their parents. Dunbar students from homes of low socioeconomic status also had substantially higher I.Q.'s than the black population at large. Special efforts were made by Dunbar teachers and counselors to tutor promising students from such backgrounds and to see that both they and their parents understood the importance of a college education, and the numerous practical details to be taken care of in order to secure college admission and financial aid. Most black high school students today get nothing resembling this kind of preparation, whether they are in all-black or in "integrated" schools.

PATTERNS OF BLACK SUCCESS

Dunbar developed and thrived during its period of academic ascendancy in almost total isolation from whites. Even as a subject of research, Dunbar was as remote from whites as if it were on Mars. It was part of a dual school system ultimately controlled by whites, but the white officials took little interest in what was going on at Dunbar, and such interest as they did manifest took such forms as trying to get the school to move in a non-academic direction and resisting the demands of Dunbar parents for calculus courses and better chemistry labs. They casually destroyed the institution as an incidental by-product of their reorganization of the Washington school system in 1954. Ironically, white liberals noticed Dunbar only after it became a typical ghetto school with all the usual problems—and even then its previous history remains wholly unknown to them. Considering the general effect of white liberals on black education, it may be that the absence of such people and their "innovative" programs should be counted among Dunbar's major advantages.

The Dunbar experience is by no means an argument for either externally imposed segregation or self-imposed separatism—and in fact the school fought against both these ideas. The founders of the school first tried to secure equal access to all public schools for all students, and only when this failed did they set about producing the best school they could for black youth. Down through the years, Dunbar teachers sought to break through the imposed insularity of a segregated society by bringing both black and white speakers, entertainers, and other cultural attractions to the school. While Dunbar promoted racial pride, it was pride in the achievements of outstanding Negroes as measured by universal standards, not special "black" achievements by special "black" standards.

There is a tendency among some white critics of the American Negro to point to particular black "success" models and ask, "Why can't the others do it?" If racial barriers and cultural handicaps did not stop men like Ralph Bunche and Edward Brooke, how can they provide a blanket excuse for welfare recipients and hell-raisers? It is no answer to say that Bunche, Brooke, and others were just "exceptions," for that amounts to nothing more than rephrasing the question. What the Dunbar history shows is the enormous importance of time, tradition, and institutional circumstances in providing the essential setting in which individual achievement can flourish. If such achievements were wholly or predominantly a matter of personal ability, so many outstanding individuals would not have come from one institution.

This concentration of black achievement in a few special settings is not limited to Dunbar. As rare as black doctorates are, empirically they are not isolated phenomena. A study of 609 Ph.D.'s awarded to Negroes in 1957–1962 showed that, while these black Ph.D.'s had attended 360 different high schools, 5.2 percent of these high schools had produced 20.8 percent of the Ph.D.'s (Dunbar was first among these high schools). A more relevant comparison would have included the vast number of black high schools whose alumni earned no Ph.D.'s during that period—but this would only have made the concentration still more extreme. Another study examined those black families in which someone had earned a doctoral degree of some sort (M.D., Ph.D., etc.) and found that the average number of doctorates per family was 2.25. If the family setting permitted someone to earn a doctorate, it generally permitted more than one to earn a doctorate. Impressionistic evidence on the backgrounds of historic black figures also suggests that black achievements have come out of circumstances very different from those which the majority of Negro Americans experience. W. E. B. DuBois grew up with aristocratic New England whites, Ralph Ellison grew up on frontier territory, George Washington Carver was raised by a German couple, and even Booker T. Washington, though "up from slavery," was in his youth the protegé of a succession of wealthy, educated, and influential whites. This in no way demeans the achievement of these men, for ultimately they had to have the ability to do what they did. But it does underline the importance of the special circumstances necessary for individuals to realize their potential—and the remoteness of these circumstances from the lives of most American Negroes.

THE PROBLEM OF DISCIPLINE

Despite the emphasis on small classes in the educational literature, Dunbar had large classes. As far back as 1877, there were 40 students per teacher, and a survey in 1953 showed Dunbar's student-teacher ratio to be higher than that of any white senior high school in Washington. This was not a matter of principle but of necessity, given the inadequate financial support the school received from the white-controlled Board of Education. Obviously, class size is less of a handicap with self-selected and highly motivated students than with average students or with students lacking self-discipline. But while the Dunbar experience is not directly generalizable to ghetto schools, it does indicate where the problem lies. There is no inherent reason why large classes cannot be educationally effective, or even psychologically inspiring. The class size at which learning breaks down and disorder sets in is a function of the attitudes brought to the situation by students and teachers.

Much contemporary discussion of teaching methods, educational philosophies, and organizational principles in the school system seems unreal in the context of the "blackboard jungle" atmosphere in many ghetto schools. While more classroom time is often devoted to trying to maintain order (or contain disorder) than to teaching, more educational literature is devoted to philosophy, politics, "black English," and in fact almost anything other than the overriding problem of reducing the chaos, disruption, and fear which can prevent any teaching method or philosophy from being effective. Yet it is not considered politic, much less chic, to discuss such things.

Although Dunbar, when it was an elite high school, had few discipline problems, its history is not wholly irrelevant here. The importance of parental attitudes and parental involvement was recognized literally from the inception of the school. Although Washington in 1870 had many Negro families who were ready and eager for a first-rate school, it also had many who were not. The recent abolition of slavery had swelled the black population of Washington with many new arrivals from Southern and border states. As of 1868, only about one third of the Negro children of the District of Columbia were attending any school. In this setting, William Syphax's admonitions to black parents to send their children to school with respect for learning and a readiness to work were very much to the point.

Black schools that have been educationally successful generally have not shared a common teaching method or educational philosophy. They have almost invariably had a high level of parental involvement. This was true throughout the ascendancy of Dunbar High School. It was also true of successful Harlem schools studied by Charles E. Silberman.[8]

THE IMPORTANCE OF PARENTAL INVOLVEMENT

I found a graphic example of this in a ghetto school I visited in Cincinnati. Although Frederick Douglass School did not attain the erstwhile academic achievements of Dunbar, it was striking because its ancient building stood in the midst of a run-down slum, with no fence around it, no bars on the windows, no graffiti, quiet halls, and an atmosphere of human relations among the staff that would have been a credit to a middle-class private school. Board of Education statistics showed its staff morale indicators (turnover, etc.) and student performance to be well ahead of what should have been expected according to the socioeconomic profile of its neighborhood. Principal Tom Murray mentioned in passing that the school had corporal punishment, and added: "The staff resisted the idea, but the parents insisted upon it." When a white principal in a black school is given the authority to administer corporal punishment at the insistence of the parents, there is clearly more here than meets the eye—particularly in an era when the very appointment of a white principal in a black school is often opposed by the community (as Murray's appointment had been). Yet, by visiting the homes of hundreds of students, by talking "straight" (even bluntly) to the parents, by involving himself in the community, this man had been able to involve the community in the school. The important question here is not whether corporal punishment is good or bad, any more than the important question about Dunbar was whether Latin was really needed. The point is that certain human relations are essential to the educational process, and when these conditions are met, then education can go forward—regardless of methods, educational philosophy, or physical plant.

Parental involvement is particularly important in black schools, for the black culture is not a permissive culture. If black kids raise hell, it is because their parents don't know or don't care, but not because of any philosophy that youths should "do their own thing." Where black parents have become involved in a school, they have sometimes urged a stricter discipline than the school was prepared to impose. Parental involvement does not mean making "community control" either an ideological dogma or a public relations ploy. Where a community has a high rate of residential turnover, "community control" can mean the unchallenged dominance of a handful of activists not accountable to any lasting constituency. What is important is the widespread involvement of individual parents as such.

The importance of individual parents is often ignored or slighted. Schemes for "open enrollment," voucher systems, or any other form of free choice by black parents of public school children invariably run into the argument that uneducated ghetto parents cannot make informed educational choices. Yet the history of Dunbar High School shows that only a relative handful of people need to understand the complexities involved in creating a first-rate education. Once they have created such an education, the others need only be able to recognize it. Generations of non-middle-class youngsters were sent to Dunbar for just this reason. Today, thousands of other non-middle-class black youngsters are being taken out of dreadful ghetto schools (created by those who presumably do understand education) and enrolled in local Catholic schools by Protestant black families. The cost of such schools is typically very low compared to other private schools, but still very high compared to ghetto incomes—and yet many black families are making this sacrifice in cities across the country. But this widespread phenomenon remains a non-event for intellectuals, just as Dunbar High School was a non-event for 85 years. To admit the possibility of widespread individual initiative on the part of those at the bottom of the socioeconomic ladder would be to threaten a whole conception of the world and of the intellectuals' own role in it.

THE DUNBAR EXAMPLE

During the 1870–1955 period, the self-selection of students freed Dunbar from the incubus of disinterested and disruptive students. After such students began entering, following the school reorganization of 1954, they destroyed the school within a few years. Various forms of self-selection can free other institutions from the hard core of disruptive and violent students, but all plans that involve freedom of choice (vouchers, open enrollment, etc.) are damned by critics as inhibiting racial integration. It is an empirical question, however, whether black youngsters will gain more educationally by separation from a hard core of hell-raisers or by integration with whites. Studies of the educational effects of integration show few gains. Yet the shibboleth of integration is still powerful enough to thwart fundamental educational reform.

The combination of historical circumstances that created Dunbar

High School can never be recreated. Some of those essential circumstances should not be recreated—for example, the racial barriers which led a scholar like Carter G. Woodson to teach at Dunbar High School, when he should have been conducting graduate seminars at a major university. Yet such historical experiences contain important lessons for the present. Dunbar did not seek "grass-roots" teachers who could "relate" to "disadvantaged" students, even though a substantial part of its students were the children of maids, messengers, and clerks. Dunbar's faculty included many "overqualified" people, in today's parlance. Almost all of its principals during its 85-year ascendancy held degrees from the leading colleges and universities in the country —not teacher's college degrees or education degrees from other institutions. They had been trained in hard intellectual fields and had been held to rigid standards, and this was reflected in the atmosphere and standards of Dunbar.

While the Dunbar experience provides some empirical refutation for currently fashionable statements about the "necessary" ingredients of good education for black children, it is not itself a universal model. Part of Dunbar's strength was that it did not try to be all things to all people. The founders of the school intended it to be an institution solely devoted to preparing black students for college and in that special role it was unsurpassed. It showed what could be done and some of the ways that it could be done; it also demonstrated that some of the presumed "prerequisites" of good education are not really essential. What is essential is to create and sustain an atmosphere of academic achievement.

Dunbar High School provides no instant formulas for use by "practical" planners. Its example suggests that instant formulas by "practical" planners may not be the way to quality education. What is needed, above all, is a sense of purpose, a faith in what can be achieved, and an appreciation of the hard work required to achieve it. As the many flaws of Dunbar indicate, it is not necessary to find ideal people or an ideal setting, but it does require a dedicated nucleus of people in a setting where their dedication can be effectual.

NOTES

1. Mary Gibson Hundley, *The Dunbar Story* (New York: Vintage Press, 1965), p. 57.

2. Rather than keeping track of a variety of changing names, we will use "Dunbar" throughout to denote each of the successive institutions continuously deriving from the high school established in 1870.

3. E. Delorus Preston, Jr., "William Syphax, A Pioneer in Negro Education in the District of Columbia," *Journal of Negro History* (October 1935), pp. 462–64.

4. Mary Church Terrell, "History of the High School for Negroes in Washington," *Journal of Negro History* (July 1917), pp. 255–56.

5. Ibid., p. 259.

6. See Thomas Sowell, *Black Education: Myths and Tragedies* (New York: David McKay Co., 1972), p. 143.

7. Hundley, op. cit., p. 31.

8. Charles E. Silberman, *Crisis in the Classroom—the Remaking of American Education* (New York: Random House, 1970).

10

Presentation to Massachusetts Legislature—March 30, 1976

James S. Coleman

I WANT TO express my pleasure at being here to address you, along with my surprise at being invited to do so. This is not the surprise of an academic scholar in being taken seriously by persons who make decisions and take action, for scholars have in recent years come to be taken very seriously in current affairs. It is rather surprise at your creation of a direct dialogue unmediated by television, newspapers, newsmagazines, or even written research reports, between those who make policy and one who carries out research which is relevant to that policy. This is a rare occasion, one which few legislatures bring about, and I want to commend the legislature of Massachusetts for doing so.

The occasion, I will assume, reflects the depth of your concern with the problem of school desegregation, the problem of bringing about an integrated society, and the problem of bringing justice and equity to all citizens of Massachusetts. I will do my utmost to respond with the seriousness and responsibility which that concern warrants.

What I will try to do in this session is to first indicate the goals that are intended to be achieved in school desegregation, then to present some research results that are relevant to certain of these goals, next to lay out what I feel are the necessary requirements for a viable policy of school integration, and finally to indicate the kinds of policies that meet those requirements. I will not, despite what the Boston Globe has to say, recommend to you specific courses of action, such as still another compulsory bussing plan. I trust that the Globe will report correctly what I have to say today; but even if it does not, the dialogue today is a direct one.

The first goal in school desegregation is that of achieving equal protection under the law for all children regardless of race. This means,
since the landmark 1954 *Brown* decision in the U.S. Supreme Court,
the elimination of de jure segregation, that is, the elimination of dual
school systems where they exist, and the elimination of official practices by school systems which bring about segregated schools. A second goal, related to the first, but distinct from it, is the goal of increasing the educational gains of disadvantaged children, particularly
minority children, black, Spanish American, and others. This goal
came to be linked to school desegregation by research results, which
showed that disadvantaged children achieved more highly on standardized tests in schools that had a middle class majority. The best
known of this research, usually referred to as the "Coleman Report,"
was carried out by myself and others in the U.S. Office of Education
under the Civil Rights Act of 1964. Since school desegregation has
become widespread, a large amount of additional research on this
topic has been carried out. I will mention briefly some of the results
of that research later.

A third goal in school desegregation is that of helping to achieve
an integrated society, one in which racial distinctions play a smaller
part than at present, and in which a person's skin color is not an overriding social characteristic. This too is related to the first goal, but
goes beyond it. It was the main impetus behind the decision to desegregate in the 1960's by school boards in many smaller northern
systems which had not practiced de jure segregation, but had residential segregation which led to extensive segregation in the schools.
Examples are: Evanston, Illinois; White Plains, New York; Ann
Arbor, Michigan; and Berkeley, California.

All three of these goals are important ones for our society to
achieve. But it is important to keep in mind these distinct goals of
school desegregation for three reasons. First, although they appear at
first glance compatible, it turns out that they are not always so, and
that sometimes actions taken to achieve one are harmful to the others.
Second, the instruments of government that are appropriate to each
of these goals are somewhat different. The courts are the appropriate
instrument, or at least the instrument of final resort, for the first;
school authorities and teachers are the appropriate instruments for the
second, with possible aid from legislative actions; and school boards,

state legislatures, and the Congress are appropriate instruments for the third. Finally, research results are differentially applicable to the three goals. They are not directly applicable to the first. Research results on what happens to children educationally, particularly disadvantaged minority children, under conditions of school segregation and desegregation are of course directly relevant to the second goal. And research results on how school desegregation affects the broader integration of society are relevant to the third goal. In particular, the effects of school desegregation on demographic changes which may strengthen or weaken the integration of society are relevant.

With these distinctions in mind, I will review briefly research results that are relevant to the second and third goals, for it is these two goals which actions of this legislature might help achieve.

THE EFFECTS OF SCHOOL DESEGREGATION ON ACHIEVEMENT OF DISADVANTAGED MINORITY CHILDREN

The so-called Coleman Report, published in 1966 under the Civil Rights Act of 1964, showed that disadvantaged children performed better on standardized tests in schools that were predominantly middle class, and that middle class children did not perform worse in schools with substantial proportions of disadvantaged children. Since there are too few middle class minority children to bring about predominantly middle class schools without racial desegregation, this result has direct implications for desegregation, implying that desegregation would improve the performance of blacks without lowering that of whites.

This result was subject to some questioning and some reanalysis. Questions concerned the possible selectivity of disadvantaged children in middle class schools, since most of the integration existing at that time was that due to residential proximity of blacks and whites. And the reanalysis showed that some portion of the apparent effect vanished when stronger controls for the social backgrounds of children were taken into account.[1] Nevertheless the research results remained, and were widely used in support of school desegregation.

Since that time, there have appeared results on the actual effects of school desegregation on achievement in particular school districts, which are more directly relevant to the issue. In general, these results can be summarized by saying that achievement benefits of school desegregation for blacks are sometimes found, sometimes not, and where they are found, are generally small, much smaller than would have been predicted from the Coleman report. David Armor, in a study of the Metco plan in the Boston area in 1972, and a review of other studies, found no benefits. Nancy St. John, in summarizing the effects for a large number of individual desegregation studies, finds erratic and small positive effects. Since her review, some other research has been similarly disappointing. An extensive study of long-term system-wide desegregation in Riverside, California finds no achievement increases, a study of Pasadena arrives at similar conclusions, and a study of bussing in Waco, Texas shows negative effects.[2] A very recent analysis of National Assessment results, released on March 17, shows what appears to be a beneficial result: although there are declines in achievement for nearly all groups throughout the country in recent years, black children in the Southeast have *increased* achievement in science since 1969. This period has been the period of greatest desegregation in the South. But the further analysis shows that this increase has been in schools that have remained all-black, just as in the integrated schools. Thus an explanation other than the racial composition of the school is necessary for these encouraging results.[3]

Altogether, the current evidence indicates that the presumed benefits of school desegregation for black achievement are sometimes present, but not uniformly so, and are small when they are found. Thus the earlier hope that school desegregation would constitute a panacea for black achievement, or contribute substantially to the goal of increasing black achievement, appears to have been misplaced.

Similarly, most of the studies mentioned earlier have found that the psychological effects (such as effects on self-esteem) and the attitudinal effects (such as interracial attitudes) of school desegregation are not uniformly in a positive direction, and are sometimes negative. Altogether, I believe we can say from the research results on the educational effects that school desegregation is seldom harmful (though where there is extensive turbulence, the short-term effects may be educationally harmful to both blacks and whites), sometimes beneficial, but not sufficiently so that school desegregation can be a major policy instrument for increasing black achievement and self-esteem.

THE DEMOGRAPHIC EFFECTS OF SCHOOL DESEGREGATION

Now I would like to turn to research results relevant to the third goal of achieving social integration. The effects that have been most extensively studied are the effects of desegregation on the racial stability of the schools, and most particularly on the loss of whites from the schools. The questions are: does this effect exist? if so, under what conditions? and what are its long-term consequences for the integration of the schools and of society?

The answers to these questions are fairly complex. First of all, it has been shown that in many small systems, when the proportion of black children in the system is not large, especially in the North and West, but also to a considerable extent in the South, desegregation does not have strong effects on loss of whites, and in fact, any effects are difficult to detect statistically. The fact that this holds true even in the South has meant that Southern desegregation, primarily in 1970, has made its schools the least segregated in the nation. Several studies have shown the absence of statistically observable effects in the North and West. Jane Mercer found this in California, and Christine Rossell found this in the North generally.[4] However, when the proportion of black children is high, then even in small districts, system-wide desegregation does have very strong effects on loss of whites from the public schools. This has been observed only in the South, for it is only there that small school systems have high proportions of blacks. Charles Clotfelter found in a study of desegregation involving system-wide racial balance in Mississippi counties that as the percentage of black children increased from 40% to 80%, the percentage of whites leaving those districts and enrolling in private schools increased from about 20% to about 90%.[5] And Luther Munford found, in another Mississippi study, that as the percentage of black children increased from 40% to 90% the percentage of whites who left the public schools in the first year increased from about 5% to about 90%. For every 10% increase in proportion of black children in those schools, an additional 16% of white children left the schools.[6] In a study of Florida countywide desegregation, Michael Giles and his associates showed that when the percentage of black children was below about 30%, the loss of whites was small. In some smaller districts in the North such as Pasadena, California and Pontiac, Michigan, where the proportion of black children was substantial then there has been substantial loss of whites as well.

I should point out that these results do not imply that whites will always escape a circumstance in which the schools are majority black. In the neighborhood in which I live in Chicago, the school has been a majority black school with a stable integrated population for 15 years. But such patterns of integrated school stability depend upon integrated neighborhood stability, they depend on continuous efforts by blacks and whites working together, and are seldom achieved by administrative or judicial fiat.

When we turn to desegregation in large cities, the picture includes an additional complexity, that is, the existence or absence of predominantly white suburbs outside the district which is desegregating. A few large cities, primarily in the South, have county-wide school districts, including all or nearly all the suburbs in the metropolitan area. These cities include Tampa, St. Petersburg, and Miami, in Florida; Charlotte, North Carolina; and Nashville, Tennessee. In these county-wide systems, all with a small proportion of black or other minority population, the loss of whites is not large (averaging about 5% in the first year of desegregation), and for those located in areas which are experiencing a population boom, as in Florida, the loss appears to be confined to the first year, with succeeding years showing the population gains characteristic of the region as a whole.

The situation, however, is quite different in central city school districts, surrounded by predominantly white suburban school districts. This is characteristic of most large cities in this country, and particularly so in the large cities of the East and Midwest. It is true to a lesser extent for medium-sized cities. Desegregation in such cities brings about a substantial loss of whites in the first year, and a continuing loss beyond the first year. The results of my own research over the past year show this. As an example, for the nine largest central-city school districts which underwent substantial desegregation between 1968 and 1974, I examined the loss of whites in years before, during and after desegregation. Two years before desegregation, the average loss was 4.1%; one year before, it was 4.8%. In the year of desegregation, it jumped to 12.4%, almost three times as great. In the four years following desegregation, it went down, but not to the pre-desegregation level: to 7.0%, 6.7%, 10.1%, and 8.1%.

In a similar tabulation, David Armor has examined these losses for the 16 cities in this country which have the following characteristics: in all of them, desegregation occurred through court order; all were in 1968 20,000 or larger in number of students; all have substantial suburbs for whites to move to, and all had a percentage of black children in the range of 20% to 50%. There was an overlap of only four cities between the nine I just described and Armor's 16. Armor found an average loss of 2% per year in the two years before desegregation, 10% in the year of desegregation and the year after, and an average loss of 7% per year in the next two years, the second and third years following desegregation. Although the cities were largely different ones, those results correspond closely to my own.

These results are serious in their demographic consequences for our large cities: for with blacks constrained within the city both by economics and by suburban residential discrimination, and whites given an additional incentive to leave by desegregation measures in the central city, the metropolitan area becomes composed of black schools in the city and white schools in the suburbs.

Even more generally, it is important to see those results in the context of broader patterns of migration that are occurring in this country. There are two major components to the current migration patterns. One is to the South and Southwest, to the "sun belt" as it has recently been called, and the other is away from major metropolitan centers. For the first time in history, the metropolitan area population, not just the central city population, has begun to decline. The movement is a movement of the segment of the population that is white, middle class, and young, the segment with most mobility. Whether this is labelled escapism, or whether it is seen as an attraction for the natural environment, it is there, and it affects most greatly the large, older urban centers of the Northeast and Midwest. They are no longer attractive to many of the young most able to move. And their moves increase the separation of blacks and whites, as they increase the decline of our older metropolitan areas.

If these trends were not serious enough, there is another aspect of the desegregation effects I have described earlier: these effects are only for the "average" city which has undergone desegregation. In a city with a high proportion of black children, then desegregation, even when it is less than full-scale racial balance, brings about a much larger loss of whites than in a city with a low proportion of blacks.

For example, I carried out a statistical analysis of desegregation in the largest central cities, and my estimates show that when there is an amount of desegregation that is sufficient to bring about a 9% loss in the first year in a district with a 25% black school population, that same amount of desegregation would bring about a 24% white loss in the first year if the district were 75% black rather than 25%. For an extreme example, in Detroit last summer, there was a court case for school desegregation. Detroit had a 75% black school system last year. The plaintiff's desegregation plan was one to create racial balance, within about 5%, in all Detroit schools. The estimates I just described, based upon large central-city desegregation which occurred between 1968 and 1973, would lead to the prediction that if the plaintiff's plan of full-scale racial balance had been adopted (which it was not) Detroit's schools would be 95% black today, that is nearly all black central-city schools and nearly all white suburban ones.

When the proportion of black children is substantial, but smaller than .75, such sharp consequences are not immediate; the effect is a snowballing one: after some whites leave, the proportion of black children is greater, leading still more whites to leave.

Boston presents an example, though far from the most extreme, of what happens when extensive desegregation is imposed in a central-city school district. In the five years before desegregation, there had been a loss of approximately 4.5% of whites per year. In 1974, when desegregation took place, there was a loss of 16.1%, over three times as great. And in 1975, the additional loss, using figures for December 31, 1975, is 15.5% if students are kept on the rolls who never came to school throughout the fall. If they are not included, the figure is even worse, a loss of 18.9% of the 1974 white enrollment—or altogether, in two years, a loss of 32% of the 1973 white enrollment, almost one-third. This had the effect of reducing the non-Spanish white student population in Boston from 57% to 41% in two years.

Altogether, then, when we look at the effects of school desegregation for the third goal, the goal of achieving social integration in America, the results are mixed. If we look at small school districts, rural areas, and countywide metropolitan districts, then extensive school desegregation, even compulsory racial balance, has not led to social segregation through a loss of whites from the schools—so long as the proportion of black children in the schools is low. Because it has not led to demographic instability, it has probably been beneficial, in both the short run and the long run, to the goal of social integration. But at the other extreme, that is in large cities, with available suburbs, and with a moderate to high proportion of black children, school desegregation, in particular compulsory racial balance, has proved disastrous to social integration, by greatly accelerating the loss of whites from the cities, and leading to racially divided metropolitan areas, with a black central city and white suburbs. The extent of this impact is not yet evident, because it is a snowballing effect, which has had only a short time to operate. But it is a policy that, carried out in the name of accomplishing the first goal of desegregation, that is, elimination of de jure segregation, acts to defeat the third goal, the goal of achieving social integration. If this policy of racial balance, ordinarily imposed by a court order, is required to overcome de jure segregation, then we confront an insoluble dilemma: an action necessary to bring about equal protection under the law for blacks and whites has the overall effect of defeating social integration among blacks and whites. However, I believe the dilemma to be a false one: that seldom if ever is compulsory racial balance in a large school system necessary to overcome de jure segregation. Rather, straightforward elimination of de jure segregation in large cities would constitute primarily a redrawing of school attendance zones to eliminate gerrymandering, and would have little impact, one way or another, on the third goal of achieving integration. That goal must be achieved by much more long range policies, involving residence at least as much as schools, policies that recognize both the needs and desires for ethnic community and those of ethnic integration. The achievement of that third goal in our metropolitan areas must involve a variety of policies, including those that attract middle class whites into the city, and those that make the suburbs available to blacks commensurate with their rising incomes.

This is not by any means to say that imposing racial balance in city schools is the only policy that has led to increasingly black central cities and white suburbs. Freeway construction, FHA mortgage policies, the inability to control crime, and other policies have been responsible as well. But there is probably no single action that has had as strong and immediate an effect in removing whites from already substantially black central cities than the policies of racial balance in the schools, where those policies have been put into effect in large central cities.

These various research results raise finally the question of what should be the characteristics of school desegregation policies if the three goals, elimination of de jure segregation, benefitting achievement of disadvantaged children, and achieving social integration, are to be realized. First, I believe it must now be recognized, although I did not at one time believe this to be so, that school desegregation is not a central instrument for achieving the second goal. It is neither necessary nor sufficient for improving the achievement of disadvantaged children. Imaginative and varied patterns of interaction with children from other social classes and ethnic groups can be an important and valuable element in education, but to paraphrase Wilson Riles, Superintendent of Schools in California, it is not necessary for a black child to sit next to a white child in order to learn.

Second, the first goal, of eliminating de jure segregation should be recognized for what it is, and as quite separate from the goal of achieving racial integration in society. Elimination of de jure segregation, properly done, will in large cities neither greatly aid nor greatly harm the racial integration of the society. By itself, it cannot be an important instrument for the latter goal in large cities where blacks and whites are largely separated by residence. When it has been used as such, it has helped defeat, rather than achieve this third goal, as I have indicated in the statistics I presented.

Third, the third goal, achieving an integrated society, is one for which government policies can be decisive, but only if the policies recognize that they require active support and implementation by ordinary families, of all racial groups: families whose actions and attitudes in the long run will determine the success of the policies. These policies must, by their very nature, be carried out primarily by legislatures, for most are outside the reach of the courts, and beyond the scope of local jurisdictions.

What I would like to suggest, then, are certain requirements that school policies should meet if they are to aid in achievement of the goal of achieving a racially integrated society.

1. Any policy should insure equal treatment for all children, regardless of race, ethnicity, or social origin.

2. Any policy designed to aid in achieving an integrated society should be one which facilitates and encourages social integration of whites, blacks, and other minorities, and one which prevents exclusion by one group of members of another; but it should allow mem-

bers of each group to be in minority or majority situations. It is not an appropriate aim of policy, for example, to "eliminate racially identifiable schools," which is a euphemism for eliminating all-black schools.

3. Any policy should not by design or consequence be punitive on families or children, whether in the name of redressing past wrongs or for other purposes. Much of the error in school desegregation policy has been the result of an unarticulated punitiveness which has no place in achieving positive social goals.

4. If a policy imposes additional constraints in order to increase the degree of racial integration in schools, it should impose those constraints on schools or school districts, and not on families or children, through arbitrary school assignment. To do the latter creates an incentive for those with money to leave the school system, either for private schools, for the suburbs, or for another metropolitan area altogether, and a disincentive for persons to move into the area. A policy should attempt to achieve integration through *increasing* the options available to families and children, not through restricting options. Such an increase is especially important for blacks and other minorities, and for low-income families, for their residential options have been severely limited through residential discrimination or economic constraints.

5. Any policy must not treat differentially city and suburbs, despite the fact that there are different school systems involved. To do so increases the relative attractiveness of the suburbs for middle class families, especially whites, and directly defeats the goal of social integration of blacks and whites.

These requirements for a policy are, taken together, quite restrictive. They imply that no political subdivision below the state can take appropriate integrative action—not a city, not a suburb, for integration must involve the metropolitan area as a whole. Thus they imply that a state legislature is one of the few arms of government that can take appropriate action. And they imply that whatever policies a legislature does impose cannot assign children to specific schools distant from their home, that is, cannot involve compulsory bussing.

I will describe a policy that meets these requirements, to illustrate what I feel is a feasible school desegregation policy. I am not recommending such a policy to you, because it would be presumptuous of me to tell you what should be done in Massachusetts.

A policy which meets these criteria would be one of educational entitlements: each child in a metropolitan area would be entitled to attend any school in the metropolitan area, whether it is in his school district or not, so long as it does not have a higher proportion of his own racial group than the school to which he would be assigned on the basis of residence. With this entitlement would go the provision of transportation, so that the plan sounds like a "voluntary bussing plan across school district lines." But it is not that, for each family and child would be able to choose either his neighborhood school or nearly any other school in the district. Every school would be required to accept out-of-attendance-zone students up to something like 15% of its total student population, a percentage small enough so that double shifts would not be required, but large enough to provide a wide opportunity for choice. State aid to education would necessarily be modified in such a way that a child's per-pupil expenditure followed him to his new district. The plan would be most important for blacks and low income families, who are excluded by economics or discrimination from certain residential areas. But it would not by any means be a one-way movement, because especially at the high school level, the city can offer specialized schools and alternative schools that a suburb cannot, schools which can attract young people from the suburbs. The plan could be described as one in which every school in the metropolitan area becomes a magnet school, for each school would be required to attract its student body. It is this aspect of such a plan, incidentally, that often makes school administrators uncomfortable with it: it is much easier to assign captive student bodies to schools than to compete for students.

Obviously, such a school desegregation plan will not "eliminate racial segregation" in the schools of the metropolitan area. But to do that is, as I have said, a wholly inappropriate and even racially discriminatory goal. It would weigh heavily upon black children, for each black would be in an extreme minority; neither blacks nor Spanish-Americans could choose to be in a school where they were in a racial majority.

This sketches the outlines of a plan which would meet the criteria that I believe are necessary if school desegregation is to aid the goal of stable racial integration in the society. It is not the only such plan, and school desegregation is not the only kind of policy that can aid integration. But it is one policy that I believe would do so. I should mention as an aside that an important litmus test of any school de-segregation policy you might develop, to determine whether its principle is a sound one, is that it be equally effective if the racial composition of the metropolitan area were reversed. If it would not, then the principle on which it is based is likely an unsound one.

I will conclude by expressing my belief that not only is it desirable for state legislatures to develop creative policies that move toward the goal of a racially integrated society; it is important that they do so. For it is in the absence of such policies that plaintiffs have often felt, and understandably so, that only by redefining de jure segregation in a very inclusive way, and only by use of the courts, could any progress toward the third goal be made. As I have indicated by the statistics I have given, those actions have in the large cities taken us instead farther from that goal rather than closer to it. It thus becomes especially important for state legislatures to initiate those policies that will aid stable social integration, and will make their cities and metropolitan areas more attractive places for families of all groups to live and raise their children.

Again, I want to express my pleasure at being here, and to commend you for creating occasions such as this, in which there can be a direct dialogue between those who make policies and one who carries out research relevant to those policies.

NOTES

1. See Marshall Smith, in F. Mosteller and D. Moynihan, *On Equality of Educational Opportunity*, Random House, 1972.

2. See David Armor, "The Evidence on Bussing," *The Public Interest*, Summer, 1972, pp. 90–126; Nancy St. John, *School Desegregation*. New York: Wiley, 1975; *Desegregation: A Longitudinal Study*. Ralph Gerard and Norman Miller, Plenum Press, 1975, and Lawrence Felice, "Mandatory Bussing and Minority Student Achievement: New Evidence and Negative Results." Unpublished paper.

3. See National Assessment of Educational Progress, "Science Achievement: Racial and Regional Trends, 1969–73." March 17, 1976.

4. See Christine Rossell, "School Desegregation and White Flight," *Political Science Quarterly*, 1976, Vol. 90, pp. 675–695, and Jane Mercer, and Terrence Scout, "The Relationship between School Desegregation and Changes in the Racial Composition of California School Districts, 1966–73." 1974.

5. Charles Clotfelter, "School Desegregation, 'Tipping,' and Private School Enrollment," *Journal of Human Resources*, VII, 1976, pp. 29–50.

6. Luther Munford, "Desegregation and Private Schools," *Social Policy*, 1976, Vol. 6, No. 4, pp. 42–45.

11

Urban Desegregation and White Flight:
A Response to Coleman

Thomas F. Pettigrew and *Robert L. Green*

THROUGH A SERIES of recent papers and press interviews, James S. Coleman, chief author of the well-known U.S. Office of Education study titled Equal Educational Opportunity, has taken the position that urban school desegregation hastens "white flight." This position has been given a great deal of publicity, because of the nation's debate over court-ordered busing and the proposed constitutional amendment to prohibit it. The time has come for a careful analysis of what it is that Coleman says and the context in which it is said.

COLEMAN'S POSITION

Our focus will be primarily upon Coleman's views and their implications, so concisely presented in his October, 1975 KAPPAN article.[1]

Coleman views with some alarm court actions intended to undo school segregation resulting from residential segregation. While he concedes the relevance of constitutional arguments raised against de jure segregation in the schools, he feels that the Fourteenth Amendment cannot be brought to bear against segregation due to "individual actions." He states that it was his intent to examine the impact of such policies, especially as they affect the tendency for white children to leave central-city schools. As he so aptly puts it, ". . . (D)esegregating a city's school system accomplished little if the school system is or becomes nearly all black, with whites in the suburbs."

In considering trends in within-system segregation, Coleman reports considerable regional differences in 1968, with the North show-ing much less overall segregation than the South. Following the fed-eral court pressure exerted in 1970, the pattern of segregation in the South in 1972 came to resemble that of the North; large cities were more segregated (by virtue of residential segregation) than smaller cities. In fact, the great overall changes in the character of Southern segregation, coupled with the lack of change in the North, led to the South's becoming the most desegregated region in the country. Cole-man cites the continued large-city/small-city segregation differential in the North and the appearance of that same pattern in the South as evidence for his contention that big-city segregation is basically de facto in nature.

His findings with respect to between-system segregation indicate a more distressing trend. In all regions, and in nearly every large metro-politan area, between-system segregation has increased. It is Cole-man's contention that such segregation is a function of white resi-dential relocation from the central cities to the suburbs, a relocation produced by court-ordered desegregation. It is Coleman's attempts to relate reductions in within-system segregation to an acceleration in white residential relocation (white flight) that constitute the pri-mary source of controversy over his findings.

In considering the co-variates of white flight—district size, propor-tion of black students in the central-city school district, between-district segregation, and within-district segregation—Coleman reports findings indicating the existence of a one-time loss of white students as a function of decreases in the level of within-district segregation. By projecting his estimates over a 10-year period, under two condi-tions (no reductions in within-system segregation and substantial re-ductions in within-system segregation), Coleman arrives at the con-clusion that desegregation efforts result in a greater loss of whites than would occur without such efforts.

From these observations, Coleman derives some policy implications. He questions how far the courts should go in attempting to reduce segregation. He indicates that it might be advisable for the courts to limit their actions to reversing the actions of administrators and the states which limit the Fourteenth Amendment rights of some citi-zens. Coleman further argues (as Southern school and public officials have argued in the past) that it might ultimately be up to local dis-tricts to decide upon an acceptable degree of segregation. And,

Coleman asserts, even beyond the responsibilities of local communities, a more fundamental issue is that of permitting individuals to make basic choices about their residence and the schools which their children attend. Coleman proposes that one approach might be to accord each child the right to attend any metropolitan school he chooses, so long as the school chosen has no higher proportion of his race than his own neighborhood school. Any other restraints, contends Coleman, should be resisted.

OTHER RELEVANT RESEARCH

Although these new Coleman results and conclusions have been widely praised in some arenas, a persistent problem hinders the uninhibited acceptance of the findings. This problem is the failure of many other researchers to replicate Coleman's findings.

Analyses by Reynolds Farley, a demographer at the University of Michigan, show results contrary to those of Coleman's analyses.[2] They show that, from 1967 to 1972, no statistically significant relationship between racial desegregation and loss of white students could be demonstrated, whether in the North or the South, in large or small urban districts. It is indeed unfortunate that Farley's research, published in January, 1975, has been forgotten in the clamor over Coleman's more "commonsense" contentions. Indeed, while Coleman has enjoyed extravagant coverage in the media, Farley has received only modest attention from the major newspapers.

In related research, Jane Mercer and Terrence Scout, sociologists at the University of California at Riverside, found no differences between 23 desegregating school districts and 67 segregated school districts in California.[3] They discovered that the two types of districts did not differ in their direction or rate of change in either student composition or in their overall population trends.

At a recent annual meeting of the American Political Science Association, Christine H. Rossell, a political scientist at Boston University, presented a paper bearing on the white flight phenomenon.[4] With desegregation data gathered by the Office for Civil Rights, U.S. Department of Health, Education, and Welfare, Rossell used a technique resembling both Farley's and Coleman's. But she went further than either in obtaining data directly from each district and for a period prior to 1967. Her analysis enables one to identify precisely which of a total of 86 Northern districts had no desegregation (26), which had varying degrees of desegregation (the remaining 60), and which of those having some degree of desegregation were under court order (only 11).

The 86 cities can be categorized into five groups: cities with court-ordered desegregation; those reassigning over 20% of their pupils (high desegregation); those reassigning between 5% and 20% (medium desegregation); those reassigning less than 5% (low desegregation); and the control group of cities in which no reassignment for desegregation took place. When comparisons are made among all of these categories, there are no significant differences in any of the comparisons between pre- and post-desegregation years with respect to a decrease in proportion of white students. The fact that not even the court-ordered districts show any particular trend is very significant, for Coleman has alleged that court-ordered busing in particular leads to white flight. Rossell, then, agrees with the earlier research showing that there has been no demonstrable relationship between desegregation and white flight.

One is led to question why there is such a discrepancy between Coleman's and Rossell's conclusions. In the first place, Coleman has never investigated which districts in his sample were under court order to desegregate. Nor did Coleman consider the HEW data for 1967 and years before. A second reason for the discrepancy is that Coleman and Rossell used different samples of cities. Rossell's sample did not include such large Southern cities as Memphis and Atlanta, but the comparably large cities in her sample did not reveal white flight as reported by Coleman for those two cities.

Another point on which Coleman and Rossell differ—and perhaps the most fundamental one—is in defining what constitutes white flight and desegregation. It would seem apparent that analysis of desegregation trends should take into account both black and white trends. For example, movements by both groups in and out of the central cities would definitely determine the realization of a "tipping point." Nevertheless, Coleman's definition of white flight considers the percentage change in absolute numbers of white students. Although this definition seems to match the current popular definition of white flight, it fails to consider the shift of whites relative to the migration of blacks. Rossell attends to changes in the enrollment of both black students and white students, and argues that her measure is educationally more meaningful.

To summarize, there is a great discrepancy between results of the studies cited here and those of Coleman's analysis. We have suggested some of the reasons why these discrepancies exist. We have ourselves carried out yet another analysis in order to investigate what we believe might well be a major reason for the obtained discrepancy: Coleman's arbitrary selection of a particular subset of large cities in his analysis. When persistently prodded, Coleman revealed that his 20 "largest" cities were in fact, not the largest cities in the nation. Furthermore, Washington was immediately dropped from the sample due to its lack of white pupils (though cities with few black pupils were retained). If the sample had really consisted of the nation's largest, it should have included the Miami-Dade, Jacksonville-Duval, Nashville-Davidson, and Fort Lauderdale–Broward districts, which are all countywide systems. Failure to include these "largest" districts enhanced Coleman's white flight effect. Indeed, in Fort Lauderdale, for instance, the number of white students increased by 39.2% during the years 1968 to 1972.

Our analysis of the white flight phenomenon considers data from all of Coleman's original "largest" cities, as well as Denver and San Francisco. We have also included Miami, Jacksonville, Fort Lauderdale and Nashville, which should have been included among the largest cities. In addition, adopting a standard cut-off size of 75,000 students added Albuquerque, Charlotte, Newark, Cincinnati, and Seattle in our sample of largest cities. Except for enlarging the sample and looking at the trend across the five years from 1968 to 1973, we have utilized Coleman's data and his loose definitions of desegregation and white flight. When we established the strength of the correlation between amount of desegregation and the percentage change in white enrollment for these cities from 1968 to 1973, we found that the positive association reported by Coleman was not obtained. In fact, our correlation was r = .30 (It is −.12 once system size and the proportion of blacks are controlled.)

It is significant to note, however, the crucial importance of two of the cities used in Coleman's analysis—Memphis and Atlanta. It is the influence of these two atypical cities of the Deep South which produced much of the positive association Coleman reported. In addition, it is interesting to note that Denver and San Francisco, which he added late in his analysis, also contribute to the strength of his positive relationship. In general, we were unable to replicate white flight results, as were Farley, Mercer and Scout, and Rossell. When we take a perspective on the five-year trend, it is fairly obvious that desegregation had no discernible effect on the loss of white students from the truly largest urban school districts. Indeed, our analysis showed that metropolitan districts such as Miami, Fort Lauderdale, Jacksonville, Tampa, Nashville, and Charlotte are rather unaffected by the phenomenon of white flight.

We would take issue with Coleman on another important methodological point. In his second analysis, in a paper titled "Trends in School Segregation, 1968–1973," presented at a one-day conference at the Urban Institute on August 4, 1975, Coleman offered a second set of prediction equations.[5] It demonstrated that when three more predictors were inserted, 60% of the variance in changes in percentage of white population could be predicted by the new eight-variable equation. This was accomplished largely by the addition of the dummy variable for the South and the interactions of change in desegregation with both interdistrict metropolitan segregation ($\triangle$ R $\times$ RSMSA) and the black proportion of students ($\triangle$ R $\times$ Prop. Black). But the point to be observed here is that the increase in predictive power is due to interaction effects, rather than being a main effect of desegregation per se. Whether desegregation will produce any discernible effect on white flight appears to be conditional upon other factors such as the percentage of black children in large central-city districts. This is an important part of his data which Coleman has not emphasized. Unfortunately, public recognition of his work usually focuses on the simple effect of desegregation on white flight.

In a recent critical review of Coleman's report, Joseph Wisenbaker of Michigan State University pointed to a number of potentially important flaws in the methodology Coleman employed in his attempt to analyze the relationship between desegregation and the decline in the proportion of white students in large-city schools.[6] In his review, Wisenbaker examined a number of points, ranging from a very crucial criticism of Coleman's unit of analysis all the way to specific averaging techniques used on the regression coefficients themselves. For example, Coleman's use of dummy (dichotomous) variables is seen as a rather ineffective attempt to control for differences among cities unrelated to those of school attendance. For them to be effective in this regard, Wisenbaker pointed out that all other variables must be assumed to be constant over the six-year period—a very stringent and probably unjustifiable assumption. Indeed, his conclusion, based on the methodological shortcomings he observed in Coleman's analyses, questioned the very usefulness of Coleman's results for anyone trying to understand the relationship between desegregation and white flight.

SIX RESULTS THAT EMERGE

We believe that it is possible, in spite of the discrepancies among these studies, all based on the same HEW data, to suggest six results which are consistent with all the analyses.

1. There has been a long-term trend of whites leaving the central cities and of blacks migrating into these areas.

2. All the studies agree that desegregation and white flight are not related in the smaller cities.

3. In the metropolitan school districts, desegregation has little or no effect on white flight.

4. Court-ordered desegregation has not had effects on white flight different from desegregation resulting from other factors, such as residential or neighborhood transition.

5. The loss of white and black students from large central-city districts is related to the proportion of black students attending those districts. In part, the "proportion black" variable is a surrogate for a range of other variables, from eroding tax bases to old housing stocks.

6. While extensive school desegregation may hasten the white flight phenomenon, particularly in the largest, nonmetropolitan districts in the South, the effect, if it obtains at all, may only be observed temporarily during the first year of desegregation, and then only for those families which have already made plans to move.

It is our contention that these conclusions directly follow a careful analysis of the data; we believe that they neither misrepresent nor go beyond the data.

PROBLEMS WITH COLEMAN'S ANALYSES
AND STATEMENTS

One of the issues surrounding Coleman's recent conclusions and the recognition given them is that of the responsibility of the social scientist to the community of scholars and with respect to the formation of public policy. In all candor, we are disappointed with the reporting practices Coleman has displayed before the eyes of the public with respect to his research.

One difficulty has been in obtaining Coleman's data. This has been a special problem in this case, since many were curious about the possible relationship between Coleman's data and his public pronouncements. When some critics questioned Coleman's conclusions and his ability to substantiate them with data, they were rather consistently subjected to ad hominem arguments quite unbecoming to all concerned.

We believe that Coleman's critics were quite appropriately interested in examining his data. From last April until August, the data that Coleman was allegedly using as a foundation for his public statements were not available in detailed form to the social science community. Further, it is interesting to note that his information, when some of it was released, was not of the substance one would require as a basis for such important policy statements. Indeed, while there have been several versions of data analysis, Coleman's conclusions have been remarkably unswerving.[7]

This changing relationship between the research data and Coleman's public statements provides even more confusion. Apparently there is no consistent and solid relationship between his data and his statements, yet he is willing to suggest repeatedly that these statements are well founded, as he does in the October, 1975 KAPPAN article. A social scientist does indeed have the right to express his political opinions, but such opinions must be clearly separable from his research findings. There is a strong tendency of the media and the public to provide the nonexistent association between opinion and data if a well-known researcher such as Coleman does not specifically disclaim this relationship.

If Coleman sees fit to express his opinions without offering good evidence for them, other social scientists should be able to express their doubts about these opinions without becoming targets for ad hominem arguments. It is our view that the social science community, least of all, needs its public image tarnished by this kind of squabbling. The means of debate among scholars should always be objective, and the time for debate should always be prior to the general release of public statements of purported research results. Indeed, one of the cardinal rules of science is that scholarship positions should be exposed to replication studies and validation by other scholars before one's conclusions are offered as established fact. Yet Coleman felt justified in abrogating this basic responsibility. It is not reasonable to assume that premature press releases will be labeled "premature" in the press, nor is it reasonable to assume that reporters will suddenly develop the·skepticism of social scientists before they send to the presses what they are given by reputable scholars.

In summary, we reach three conclusions. First, there are serious problems with the "research" which resulted in Coleman's much-publicized finding that school desegregation in the "largest" urban districts is counterproductive because it leads to massive white flight. Not surprisingly, other major studies utilizing much the same data but a variety of methods fail to replicate Coleman's key finding.

Second, there is only a tenuous connection at best between Coleman's research results and Coleman's antibusing political opinions. His own findings, as well as those of other researchers, argue strongly for metropolitan approaches to school desegregation, but he stoutly resists this direction in court appearances, Senate testimony, and his speech at an antibusing conference in Louisville, last December.

Finally, the whole episode raises difficult problems concerning the responsible influence of social science on public policy. Lacking both peer review and cross-examination, campaigns through the mass media are surely one of the least desirable means for social scientists to convey the policy implications of their research.

Notes

1. James S. Coleman, "Racial Segregation in the Schools: New Research with New Policy Implication," *Phi Delta Kappan*, October, 1975, pp. 75–78.

2. Reynolds Farley, "Racial Integration in the Public Schools, 1967 to 1972: Assessing the Effects of Governmental Policies," *Sociological Focus*, January, 1975, pp. 3–26; idem, "School Integration and White Flight" (Paper delivered at the Symposium on School Desegregation and White Flight held at the Brookings Institution, Washington, D.C., August 15, 1975).

3. Jane R. Mercer and Terrence M. Scout, "The Relationship Between School Desegregation and Changes in the Racial Composition of California School Districts, 1963–73" (unpublished). Sociology Department, University of California, Riverside, 1974, p. 28.

4. Christine H. Rossell, "The Political and Social Impact of School Desegregation Policy: A Preliminary Report" (Paper presented at the

annual meeting of the American Political Science Association, September 4, 1975, San Francisco, Calif.); idem, "The Effect of School Desegregation on White Flight." *Political Science Quarterly*, Winter, 1976, p. 92.

5. James S. Coleman, Sara D. Kelly and John Moore, "Recent Trends in School Segregation, 1968–1973" (unpublished second version, July 28, 1975, Urban Institute, Washington, D.C.).

6. For a full description of this analysis, see Joseph M. Wisenbaker, "A Critique of Trends in School Segregation 1968–1973" (unpublished paper prepared for the College of Urban Development, Michigan State University).

7. James S. Coleman, Sara D. Kelly, and John Moore, "Recent Trends in School Integration, 1968–1973" (unpublished first version presented at the annual meeting of the American Educational Research Association, April 2, 1975, Washington, D.C.); idem, "Recent Trends in School Integration, 1968–1973" (unpublished second version, July 28, 1975, Urban Institute, Washington, D.C.); idem, "Recent Trends in School Integration, 1968–1973" (unpublished third revision, August 15, 1975, Urban Institute, Washington, D.C.); idem, "Recent Trends in School Integration, 1968–1973" (unpublished fourth revision, August, 1975, Urban Institute, Washington, D.C.).

12

Desegregation
and Academic Achievement

Robert L. Crain and *Rita E. Mahard*

WHEN THE Supreme Court ruled that segregated schools were unconstitutional in 1954, many educators assumed that desegregation would bring with it improved education for black students. The first major study of the effects of desegregation on black education (the Coleman Report, carried out in 1966) showed that desegregation was beneficial—with whom one went to school was more important than the facilities and teaching materials in the school. Coleman showed that black students attending predominantly white schools had higher achievement test scores than black students of the same family background in segregated schools. The study also showed that there was no evidence that white student achievement suffered as a result of attending school with blacks.

However, most of the students surveyed by Coleman were in "naturally" integrated schools, not schools which had been desegregated with a desegregation plan. Since Coleman, a number of studies have been made of specific desegregation plans. Researchers quickly arrived at a consensus on the second of Coleman's findings—white student achievement almost never went down following desegregation and in some cases it improved. But the Coleman Report's other

This paper was prepared especially for the Illinois Office of Education, Joseph M. Cronin, Superintendent. The authors wish to thank the Ford Foundation which provided support for the preparation of this paper. The research results reported here are described in more detail and the individual studies are referenced in "Desegregation and Black Achievement" by Robert L. Crain and Rita E. Mahard, *Law and Contemporary Problems* 42, no. 2 (Spring 1978).

conclusion—that black student achievement was higher in white schools and that, therefore, desegregation would benefit blacks educationally—became a subject of controversy. In 1972, David Armor published a study of some of the research on "busing," arguing that the black achievement gains were at most trivial and certainly not worth the effort that desegregation required. Other researchers disagreed with Armor and the debate has raged ever since.

In an effort to obtain a clearer understanding of the desegregation minority achievement relationship, the National Review Panel on School Desegregation Research, supported by the National Institute of Education and the Ford Foundation, commissioned us to review all the research that has been done on this question. We found 73 different studies of specific desegregation plans in all parts of the United States—ranging from Armor's study of a voluntary program for black students going into the suburban schools surrounding Boston to the Berkeley School District's evaluation of a mandatory school pairing plan.

The results of those 73 studies are summarized in the table below.

Number of Studies Showing Black Achievement Gain from Desegregation	40
Number of Studies Showing No Black Achievement Effect from Desegregation	21
Number of Studies Showing Black Achievement Loss from Desegregation	12
	—
Total Number of Studies	73

The table shows two things. First, we think the table warns us that desegregation is not fool-proof. Like other types of educational change, desegregation can be done well or badly. If it is not done well, there is no reason to expect black achievement to improve and there is the possibility that it may suffer. But second, our data support the original Coleman finding—desegregation usually is an effective way to increase black student achievement. Most of the studies show black achievement gains. Only 12 indicate a loss in black achievement and even this seems exaggerated—in some of these cases, we think the studies were done incorrectly. Positive results far outnumber negative ones. In summary, desegregation works in achievement terms—usually raising black achievement and rarely harming white achievement.

Why does desegregation raise black achievement? The research points to several answers: because formerly white schools sometimes have better facilities, because a mixture of social classes is educationally beneficial, and because blacks profit from the opportunity to attend schools with whites.

DESEGREGATION RAISES ACHIEVEMENT BY PROVIDING BETTER SCHOOL FACILITIES

Frank Williams studied what happened when a number of black students were allowed to transfer from a small rural black school in Florida to the modern comprehensive high school which whites had been attending. When these students transferred in the tenth grade, they scored the same in verbal IQ and achievement as the students remaining in the black school. By the end of the twelfth grade, the black students in the two schools still had the same verbal IQ scores, but the desegregated black students were now scoring about 60 points higher on a test similar to the quantitative aptitude portion of the SAT. In achievement test scores, the differences were even more striking. In English, the desegregated black students scored three full grade levels higher than the students who remained behind in the black school—they had learned more than twice as much in the three years since they had left the black school. Throughout the rural south, desegregation meant the closing of small and inadequate black schools like the one Williams studied. So in at least a few of the studies we reviewed, the reason for the achievement gain was obvious —desegregation meant that blacks could escape inferior schools.

But we think that simple improvements in school quality are not the main reason why desegregation raises achievement. If it were, a large compensatory education program could obtain the same results with less community disruption. Compensatory education does help low-income students. The many evaluations of compensatory education are not as consistently favorable as the results we have seen for desegregation, but the very best studies have found compensatory programs to be effective. Compensatory education works because it provides more teachers, new curriculum materials, and additional training for teachers so that they can learn new classroom techniques. Desegregation works, we think, for a completely different set of reasons. Desegregation and compensatory education are complementary to each other, not substitutes.

DESEGREGATION RAISES ACHIEVEMENT BY PROVIDING A MIXTURE OF SOCIAL CLASSES

In many cases, desegregation helps because lower-income black students are brought together with higher-income white students. This sort of "socioeconomic integration" benefits the poorer students (and would presumably benefit white students from low-income families as well) for several reasons.

With high-income students in the classroom, the teacher will maintain a faster pace and cover more material. Teachers will set higher goals and will, by implication, expect more from the black students. A number of research studies have shown that when teachers have high (or low) academic expectations, student performance lives up (or down) to those expectations. We suspect that even the best teachers in segregated low-income or black schools come to expect less of their students. If a school is known as a low-income black school, everyone expects achievement to be low, and low performance becomes a self-fulfilling prophecy. It may be for this reason that the Supreme Court, in one of its famous decisions about school desegregation, said that a desegregation plan is not finished until there are no " 'white' schools and no 'black' schools—just schools."

Finally, low-income students tend naturally to fall in with the way the higher income students in the classroom do things. If more students in the school are well disciplined, anxious to do the work that is expected of them and planning to go on to college, the lower-income students in the classroom are likely to behave in the same way. Studies have frequently found that low-income students (both white and black) who attend higher-income schools are more likely to go to college than those in slum schools. A recent study has found that northern blacks who graduate from predominantly white high schools are nearly twice as likely to succeed in college compared to blacks of similar incomes from black high schools.

DESEGREGATION RAISES ACHIEVEMENT BY BRINGING WHITES AND BLACKS TOGETHER

We suspect that there is a third reason why desegregation benefits black students. Desegregation works because it eliminates the psychological damage done by segregation.

The Supreme Court said in 1954, that segregated schools teach blacks to think of themselves as inferior: "To separate (black children) from others of similar age and qualifications solely because of their race generates a feeling of inferiority as to their status in the community that may affect their hearts and minds in a way unlikely ever to be undone." Martin Luther King, Jr. made the same point when he wrote, "It is sometimes more difficult to determine which are the deepest wounds, the physical or the psychological." He writes of blacks facing a "color shock" which creates a "fatiguing, wearisome hopelessness."[1] If King and the Supreme Court are right, then a desegregated school is a symbol of racial equality which has considerable impact on student motivation.

It is well known that black students do not achieve as well as white students. But we must bear in mind that this does *not* mean that every black student performs worse than every white student—in the classroom some black students will excel, and the average black student will find that he outperforms many of the whites in the classroom. Black students know that sooner or later they are going to have to "make it" in a world where most people are white. Finding out that they can make it is a boost in self-confidence that cannot be provided in a segregated school, no matter how good the curriculum or the teacher.

NECESSARY CONDITIONS FOR
EFFECTIVE DESEGREGATION

In reviewing this research we have also learned something about why desegregation sometimes fails to raise black achievement. The research points to four factors that a school should be concerned about when beginning desegregation.

1. Teachers must be responsive. Several studies have shown that when teachers are unsympathetic to desegregation or expect black students to perform poorly, black achievement suffers. Teachers need help. The school should provide an adequate in-service program for the staff so that they will know what to expect from desegregation and will learn to handle their own feelings about desegregation.

2. The curriculum must be adapted to meet the needs of all students. In many schools desegregation has been seen as an opportunity to undertake the educational improvements that were not possible before. Goldsboro, North Carolina, drastically overhauled the schools, and instituted a program of individualized instruction which raised

both black and white achievement. Today, schools frequently receive additional federal funds because of desegregation, funds which can be used to develop individualized instruction in elementary schools and increased offerings in secondary schools. Many elementary school teachers are experimenting with some of the new teaching techniques which minimize individual competition among students and encourage cooperative learning. One of the interesting findings in our review is that voluntary desegregation is not more effective than mandatory desegregation—mandatory desegregation more often results in achievement gains for black students. We suspect that one reason for this is that mandatory plans are more often accompanied by widespread in-service training for teachers and major curriculum revision.

3. Educational achievement in a desegregated school depends upon good race relations. Good race relations must be the number one priority in the school. Adequately prepared and committed teachers are part of the story; a well-designed program of extracurricular activities involving all students and encouraging student cooperation in racially mixed groups is an important second part. Several studies have shown that the better the quality of race relations the higher the achievement of black students.

Researchers agree that these necessary conditions for desegregation —receptive teachers, an adequate curriculum, and a serious effort to establish good race relations—depend upon leadership. Within the school building, the principal's behavior is the key to successful desegregation. A principal who plans for desegregation and lets the staff know that desegregation can and will work makes all the difference.

In some cities, desegregation does not begin until upper elementary school or even junior high school. While this is no doubt better than no desegregation at all, our review shows most clearly that successful desegregation must begin in the earliest possible grade. There are several reasons for this. First, race relations is a much simpler problem in the early elementary grades and most difficult in junior high school. Students who enter junior high school without prior desegregation experience have a difficult time. Second, students who are shifted after the first grade find both their educational and social environment disrupted. Having adjusted to one school in the early elementary grades, they must readjust to a different school and to new friends in the later years of elementary school. This change in the child's social environment hurts educational growth. Switching from one curriculum to another may also be disruptive. One study showed that even postponing desegregation until the second grade caused problems. Students who volunteered to transfer from a Newark ghetto school to a suburban school in first grade made phenomenal growth in both reading and math—more than double the growth of a matched group of students who remained behind in ghetto schools. The second graders who transferred showed the same high rate of growth in reading, but actually lost ground in mathematics compared to segregated students. The reason? The suburban school was using a "new math" curriculum. The first graders had no math to relearn, and adjusted easily. But the second graders had some difficulties, having already spent one year learning "old math."

There is much we still do not understand about desegregation. But the work that has been done across the United States has taught us not only that desegregation can raise black achievement, but that it usually does. We have also learned some of the basic necessities for a desegregation plan which will succeed in making equality of educational opportunity a reality instead of a slogan.

Notes

1. Martin Luther King, Jr.: *Where Do We Go From Here: Chaos or Community?* Harper and Row, 1967. The text of the Supreme Court Decision is reprinted in Kenneth L. Clark, *Prejudice and Your Child* (Beacon Press, 1959).

13

The Role of the Magnet School
in Integration

John R. Vannoni

IN AN AGE when conservatives doom all desegregation efforts—voluntary or compulsory—to fail, while liberals attack magnet schools as a form of elite tokenism, the two-year-old Philadelphia High School for the Creative and Performing Arts, conceived by Superintendent Michael P. Marcase, has been quietly providing a quality integrated education for hundreds of students and has a waiting list that defies the conventional wisdoms and the theories of experts on all sides.

With the assistance offered by Title VII of the Emergency School Aid Act, the School District of Philadelphia has fashioned a desegregation vehicle in the form of a magnet school which has become the pilot for other magnet school projects now being planned. A proposal for a magnet high school, using creative and performing arts as the specialty, was developed by the School District's Federal Programs Office and Office of Community Affairs to address the needs of students at the secondary level for a unique, individualized educational experience not presently available in existing schools and to use an interdisciplinary approach to the arts. For example, major periods in world history are studied simultaneously in art, music, drama, dance, and creative writing. In essence, the teaching of the arts is unified and coordinated with the basic curricula. The school is located in a culturally concentrated area, surrounded by art and music colleges, museums, the Academy of Music, theaters, and libraries, making it readily possible to program independent study, as well as advanced study in other institutions. The curricula are reflective of the multi-ethnic, multiracial composition of the school and community.

As a result of this program, students reach as high a level of competency and creativity in the arts as they are capable of reaching, given their prior experience and training, their talents, and their ages. At the same time racial isolation is reduced among students through the development of a mutual interest in the arts.

The funds requested in the proposal were for supplementary services to provide unique educational experiences for three hundred minority and majority students. The School District of Philadelphia provided basic educational services to the students, as well as making available in this program key curricular, supportive and other administrative personnel without cost.

It began with $307,000 in federal money and $216,000 from the school district. As a magnet school designed to draw a diverse student body from all parts of the city, 300 freshmen and sophomores were selected from more than 1,000 applicants from at least a hundred city public and parochial schools—plus 200 suburban students, who were excluded under the terms of the grant. There were 180 whites, 105 blacks, and 15 with Spanish or other minority surnames, reflecting precisely the racial balance of Philadelphia in the 1970 census. This was no easy trick given the racially isolated pattern of the city's neighborhoods and 1976–77 public school enrollment data which showed 62.2 percent black, 31.8 percent white, 5.5 percent Spanish-surnamed, and 0.5 percent American Indian/Oriental students.

A review of the racial composition of students attending the various types of schools from grades one to twelve indicated a strong racial imbalance. A careful review of the racial composition of schools also indicated a high degree of racial isolation. A count of the percentages of black students enrolled in each of the regular high schools indicated that eighteen schools had more than 66 percent black students, six schools had less than a 33 percent population of black students, and eight schools fell between 34 percent and 66 percent. Thus twenty-four of thirty-two of the public high schools in Philadelphia (or 75 percent of them) tended toward minority-group isolation.

In the Philadelphia public schools, of the 12,472 teachers, 63 percent are white, 36 percent black, and 1 percent are other minorities. In the Archdiocesan Schools of Philadelphia, of the 3,316 teachers, less than 3 percent are of any minority group. Both of these school systems agreed to cooperate in the development of this magnet school program. Large numbers of students, because of their housing patterns, attend schools with students of the same racial and ethnic background. Consequently, opportunities for interacting, communicating, or gaining even a superficial understanding of other ethnic groups are meager.

To select a student body, brochures of information regarding the schools' program, its opening, and the application procedure, and a copy of the application were distributed throughout the system. Ads containing copies of the application and information on program and curriculum at the new school were placed in all of the major newspapers in Philadelphia.

Applications were received from public and private school students, including the parochial school students from the Archdiocese of Philadelphia and from the suburbs. Every section of the city was represented. To the extent that the school was to integrate, desegregate, move students geographically, and remove students from environments of minority isolation, Philadelphia's first magnet high school was a success.

City-wide advertisements through all media (bilingual included) were distributed to the various district offices and nonpublic schools for distribution to all schools. The responses to these applications were reviewed and a selection process utilized based upon race, sex, interest, and differing levels of achievement. While the school district grappled with the selection of a site, the principal had the task of program promotion, student recruitment, teacher selection, and the structuring of a nondiscriminatory means of selecting students with an interest in the arts that would yield the proper racial percentages as required by federal guidelines. In other words, he was responsible for establishing the mechanics of racially controlled admissions in such a manner as to circumvent the usual controversy over such a policy.

The fact that the school was considered experimental helped to avoid some of that controversy. Both parents and educators seemed interested in the whole idea and for the most part were encouraging. And there were those who simply took a wait-and-see attitude hoping that the end would justify the means.

At any rate, program applications were sent to all schools with ninth and tenth grade students, and dates were set for student selection through a modified audition or demonstration of interest technique. Academic criteria were not used in student selection. All students were told in advance what they were to do to demonstrate their interest in music, art, dance, drama, or creative writing. Some students were accomplished and some were not. It was artistic potential and not professional polish that the school was seeking. Students were judged by teachers and professionals in the arts. All students were rated and ranked. They were then placed in racial categories and selected on the basis of federal guidelines as stated in the grant. Those students who were not immediately accepted were placed on waiting lists within racial categories to be called up as replacements for students who might either leave or be dropped from the program.

For the students who were admitted, the school day was one period longer than the school day in standard comprehensive high schools. Students in the Philadelphia High School for Creative and Performing Arts had to take four periods a day in academic subjects as well as three periods a day in their art major.

In addition to selecting a racially balanced staff, the principal attempted, through exams held by the Division of Personnel, to select arts teachers with extensive backgrounds both in education and professionally, outside the field of education. Teachers of academic subjects with backgrounds, experiences, and accomplishments in the arts were also sought through examination.

In-service training was developed and implemented to provide instruction for staff in curriculum development and to develop awareness and appreciation of the school and community's multiethnic character, while participation by the community (parents, students, and representatives from the arts) in the decision-making aspects of the educational process was encouraged and maintained.

Other factors were considered in creating a magnet school which would successfully attract and hold interested children of mixed racial groups from the diverse geographical areas of the city, among them

pupil safety to and from school and within the school;
safe and convenient transportation from the student's neighborhood to the site or sites;
earning a reputation for quality because the aspects of the program offered would be unique and unavailable in the regular schools.

Staff for the school were selected to meet the criteria for integration and for teaching in the special program. Recruitment of staff began in November 1977, and staff were involved in planning, developing curriculum, community meetings, and media presentation for the model school, as well as asked to provide a significant degree of individualization of instruction characteristic of the creative and performing arts. Staff development has been a continuing process since the school's inception.

The school offers programs in music, art, drama, dance, and creative writing. Music, art, and drama are course offerings at many other high schools; however, in no case is there any attempt to provide a specialty in one of these areas while at the same time providing an interdisciplinary relationship with other cultural areas and aiming

a. to eliminate minority-group isolation and discrimination among the students and faculty of the school;
b. to use every possible strategy and acceptable procedure to foster interracial and intercultural activities and exposure;
c. to provide a superior educational program to interested students of both minority and majority groups in order that students would be able to work together on an equal basis;
d. to increase racial and ethnic awareness by curricular activities which highlight interdependence, cooperation, and group accomplishment;
e. to document the degree of interracial and intercultural contacts, the nature of these relationships, and their impact on pupils; and
f. to show at least one month's achievement gain for every month in the program for 75 percent of the students participating in the magnet school in reading and/or mathematics skills, with attendance a control factor.

The site location had to lend itself well to the specialty of the school. It also had to be desirable enough to attract white students from all parts of the city, to be accessible by public transportation, and most certainly had to be in racially and ethnically neutral territory, hence center city Philadelphia was chosen. There were no public schools available in center city, however; therefore space had to be leased or rented. The Philadelphia College of Art (PCA), located on Broad and Spruce Streets, seemed to be the perfect location. First of all there was PCA itself, and just next door there was the College for Performing Arts and the Shubert Theater, and down the street there was the Academy of Music, and around the corner there was the New Locust Street Theater and the Opera Company of Philadelphia and so on.

Students can travel from the most remote locations in the city to the school's front door by bus or subway with rail and trolley car transportation within easy walking distance, and students attending the school are able to purchase tokens at a reduced rate. And so the School District of Philadelphia rented the sixteenth, seventeenth, and eighteenth floors from PCA in the hope that the anticipated enrollment of 600 students two years hence would be able to live and learn in integrated harmony.

A quality integrated education is not something that occurs by chance. Instead, planning, involving all persons affected (parents, students, other community members, all levels of the educational staff), a diversity of course selections, and carefully selected staff are among the salient considerations in achieving this goal. In addition, past experience has shown that for innovative programs, the teacher-pupil ratio should not exceed twenty-five to one. Perhaps the single most important person in assuring the success of any new program is the educational leader of the school. Thus the principal must be philosophically committed to planning and implementing superior educational curricula for a multiethnic population.

It was the feeling of both the federal and local agencies that in order for the school to be a success, it would have to succeed at the very outset or it would more than likely not succeed at all, as has been the case with many magnet programs. It was also the feeling of all involved in the design of the program that the magnet concept had a far better chance of achieving desegregation as a complete school unto itself than it would ever have had as a program housed within an existing senior high school.

It was the original intention of the School District of Philadelphia's Federal Programs Office and the Office of Desegregation to have the school population approximate the racial profile of the city's population. The federal government, however, set the guidelines for Philadelphia at not less than 20 percent nor more than 50 percent total minority students, stating that more than 50 percent minority students would be to reestablish a trend toward minority isolation. As it turned out, the student enrollment for the first school year (which was actually a half year—February to June) was 53 percent white, 42 percent black, and 5 percent Spanish-speaking and other minorities. These percentages remained constant for the remainder of the school year.

Despite physical plant conditions that were anything but ideal in the first semester of the school's operation, both teachers and students seemed to thrive in their new environment. Not only did the school achieve and maintain a desegregated environment, but the students endorsed it with an average daily attendance of 93 percent for the February-to-June term. Attendance for the month of March soared to 96 percent. The response of parental interest in school activities has been overwhelming. Attendance at meetings, volunteers for committees, turnouts at performances, comments, criticism, phone calls, and commendations have all been experienced in abundance.

Citizens throughout the city in all walks of life (arts, politics, education) are being organized into a Friends of the High School for the Creative and Performing Arts by a group of interested (as well as integrated) individuals in the arts. Their organization and response to desegregation and the arts high school idea has also been encouraging and gratifying to the program and the school district as well.

In 1978–79 the High School for the Creative and Performing Arts had 500 students: 54 percent white, 41 percent black, and 5 percent Spanish-speaking or other minorities. Our facility has greatly improved, and we have even more interaction with the city's cultural institutions.

CONCLUSIONS

Magnet programs for the purpose of achieving desegregation in the city of Philadelphia have not fared well to date. These magnet programs for the most part are usually placed in existing standard comprehensive senior high schools. They have little to say about their location, must share existing staff, budget, and rostering, and are completely dependent upon the host school for their every need. Magnet schools, however, because of their very independence and singleness of purpose, have a much better chance of surviving and have survived.

Philadelphia has other magnet or magnet-type schools which are successful as magnets in that they draw students from all over the city, but none of them were established for desegregation purposes. The High School for the Creative and Performing Arts is the first magnet school in Philadelphia to be implemented specifically for voluntary desegregation. Its present success has led to other magnet schools being considered for the future.

Apparently the students in attendance at the High School for Creative and Performing Arts feel something positive for the school and its philosophy; else why would attendance be so phenomenally good?

Perhaps the message here is too obvious for jaundiced adult and professional eyes to perceive. It may be that the students are here because this is where they want to be and that the universal appeal of the program is what is helping to make it desegregated, or integrated. Perhaps we should permit young people the right to make more of their own choices regarding their academic destinies. Perhaps the purity and positiveness of their motives and motivation could accomplish far more naturally and normally than we in education, law, or politics can ever achieve legally. Clearly, the need for education leaders to make desegregation attractive and worthwhile rather than only a response to court orders and other pressures has been underscored by the success of this school. *Philadelphia Inquirer* reporter Maryanne Conheim (February 23, 1978) interviewed fourteen-year-old Staci Harris and learned that she had left her friends and the comforts of her neighborhood school to attend the new magnet school.

"It was my idea to come here," she said. "I've been dancing for six years. When I heard you could major in what you do best, I wanted to try it out."

Another student, Julie Rappaport, a freshman cello player who transferred from the (private) Germantown Friends School, told the reporter, "The whole thing is an experiment. I wanted a different atmosphere, with more emphasis on the arts. Being downtown is what I like best."

It is doubtful that interest-oriented and/or magnet schools are the miracle cure we are looking for to remedy all of our desegregation needs. Neither is it likely that we can create a great many such schools. Based, however, on the experience of the first two years at Philadelphia's High School for the Creative and Performing Arts and the prognosis for the next year, it would seem that there is something to be learned here. Schools with desirable programs in desirable locations which parents and students readily recognize as providing an enriched education could very well achieve integration.

14
METCO:
A Voluntary Desegregation Option

Horace Seldon

IN THE METROPOLITAN Boston area there is a voluntary program which transports by bus about three thousand students from Boston to 185 schools in thirty-seven suburban communities on a daily basis. The Metropolitan Council for Educational Opportunity, Inc. (METCO), is a private, nonprofit, voluntary association which was begun in 1966 by urban and suburban educators and parents. The stated purposes of METCO at that time hold true today:

1. to provide the opportunity for an integrated public school education for urban black and other minority children from racially imbalanced schools in Boston by placing them in suburban schools;
2. to provide a new learning experience for suburban children;
3. to provide closer understanding and cooperation between urban and suburban parents and other citizens in the Metropolitan area.

Originally funded by the federal government and foundation grants, the METCO program has grown steadily from its original 220 students and found wide enough approval so that it has been funded by the state since 1968. Funds are now granted by the legislature through the State Department of Education and allocated to the participating communities to provide educational services for the METCO students. The participating school systems reimburse METCO for its administrative expenses. Although METCO provides a specific set of services to the commonwealth for which it is reimbursed, it remains a private organization.

The governing body of METCO is a board of directors made up of interested citizens, parents, and educators from both Boston and suburban towns which receive METCO students. METCO accepts students, negotiates with the participating schools for student spaces, and sets up bus routes for the students. The selection of students is on a first-come-first-served basis, and efforts are made to find the best schools and services for each applicant.

The METCO board has made it clear that it does not exist to "solve" the racial imbalance of Boston's schools. It is the board's policy to serve as many of Boston's minority children as is educationally sound, as long as they volunteer to participate. METCO will expand in school systems which volunteer to participate to the extent deemed feasible by the board, and METCO will work with these schools to provide a good environment for the children placed in them.

Providing a good educational environment for the children involved means that the METCO staff continues to work hard in these areas of concern: (1) the development of black studies programs and incorporation of multicultural perspectives into curriculum; (2) the hiring of black and other minority staff in the schools; (3) provision of tutoring and special counseling services; and (4) finding ways to deal with the misunderstandings, hostilities, and vagaries within the METCO program—including the buses, and sometimes their drivers.

At the central office of METCO, located in Boston, a small staff works out of an old and modestly equipped building providing services directly to schools which receive METCO students, to the students themselves, and to parents. The staff at METCO is made up of about twenty-five people including administrators, psychologists, social workers, guidance counselors, community liaison team, a tutorial coordinator, recruitment specialist, and transportation director. Funding limitations in recent years have cut that staff to a bare-bones operation, and staff members are burdened even to keep in liaison with the 185 participating schools. The METCO office is alive with activity from early morning when buses begin to roll until very late at night when METCO parent groups meet, sometimes involving citizens from the host towns.

The role of the METCO coordinator is an important one. The

coordinator works in the receiving town and is employed by the school system of that town but has responsibilities toward METCO. The academic, social, and emotional life of the students is the coordinator's major responsibility. Coordinators serve as liaison between the METCO staff and the schools regarding all matters concerning the METCO program and the students. On the administrative level the coordinator is involved directly with the preparation and implementation of the METCO budget and overall program proposal submitted to the State Department of Education. The coordinator organizes host families in the receiving community and assists in the administration and evaluation of any special programs and the whole METCO program at the local level.

A unique characteristic of METCO is the manner in which minority parents and their children and the parents and children in the suburban METCO communities participate in the program. METCO parents are represented on the board of directors, and they meet periodically with the coordinators from the schools their children attend. There is a council of METCO parents which has been effective in lobbying, raising money for student scholarships, and maintaining active communication with the METCO staff.

In the METCO schools' communities, resident families volunteer to serve as "host families" and are paired with a METCO family in the city. The host family's chief role is to provide a "home away from home" for METCO students. In most cases the students travel many miles to attend school, and in emergencies (like sickness or transportation failure) they can turn to their host families for help. Warm personal relationships have developed between families in many cases, far exceeding METCO expectations. Further, many white students have developed close friendships with black METCO students—often the first black people they have ever met as peers. White children have been invited for weekends with their black friends' families, thus providing for many of them an experience of black family and community which their parents, living more conventionally segregated lives, have been denied. Family contacts are frequent. Innumerable social and educational gatherings have been organized between parents' groups involved in METCO.

The students have their own organization. Called the Student Council, its main purpose is to provide support for METCO students through maintaining communication among students in all communities. In this effort it sponsors educational and social events, a yearbook, and the METCO newsletter, *Images*.

GROWTH OF METCO

METCO began in 1966 with 220 students registered and expanded to a program involving 3,071 students by 1977. In 1968 the program included the city of Springfield and some of its suburban neighbors, but to the present this portion of METCO remains small, involving less than two hundred students. From 1970 to 1974 the program in Boston expanded at a yearly rate of about two hundred students. Major expansions came in 1974, 1975, and 1976, but since then growth has been small due to limited state funding. Being dependent upon state funds, METCO is subject to the political winds and financial fortunes of the state. When budget cuts are voted in the legislature, METCO experiences the same difficulty that other educational and human services programs face along with the additional hostility of those who are eager for any opportunity to cut back on what is seen as something that benefits black people.

METCO GRADUATES

One of the benefits of the METCO program for its black students is the expansion of educational opportunities beyond high school, and consequently the opening of wider career options. In 1978 194 METCO students graduated from high school in the various communities. Eighty-five percent of those graduates are slated to continue some kind of higher education. There is a wide variety of colleges and universities included in those to which graduates will advance: Brandeis University, Holy Cross, Emmanuel College, Simmons College, Arizona State, Bowdoin, Springfield College, University of Hartford are examples. Notable also is an increase in the number of METCO graduates who will be attending primarily black or all-black institutions such as Morehouse, Lincoln, and Fisk.

In 1978 graduations marked the first time since the inception of METCO that METCO students have received awards *granted within the host communities.* Previously METCO students have received awards given by METCO itself or through some other agency not a part of the local school system, but 1978 marks the first time these "host town" awards have gone to METCO students. There is some hope that this indicates an increased acceptance of METCO students as "belonging to" the receiving system and town. In one town for instance, out of twenty graduating METCO seniors there were six who received "local" awards; fourteen of those graduates will go on to higher education.

BENEFITS OF METCO FOR MINORITIES

The fact that METCO has experienced growth to the extent it has, with three thousand students now enrolled in the program, with an additional number well over three thousand on a waiting list, indicates that it is a program highly valued by minority people in Boston. Without a great many in-depth interviews or a widely distributed response document it would be insane to try to recount here all of the reasons to be found for the high value which a large number of black people place on METCO. Some of the reasons why it is valued so highly certainly are included in the following:

1. *The high rate of graduates going to further education* is important to a lot of people. There are some who will argue that this is part of the proof that the education provided in the suburban schools is better than that available to students in Boston. Others will counter by saying it is not an indicator of better education but simply indicates that it may be easier to gain entrance to more schools with a diploma from some suburban systems than from Boston. Even that last statement is a highly debatable one. It may never be possible to have research that will produce data to definitively answer the question about where a student receives the "better" education. In any event the high rate of youngsters going on to college is part of what leads at least to a perception among a lot of minority parents that participation in METCO will open more and new doors for their children.

2. There is a value shared by some minority parents who want for their children *an experience of meeting white children in a peer relationship*. Some may value this primarily as an integration experience. Others recognize that it is important for their children to meet white children and their parents who are or may someday be in positions of influence, where knowing them may open doors to employ-

ment and other opportunities. Not everyone in the suburban communities is in such a position of influence, but many are, and minority parents know that it is often "who you know" that widens opportunities for life choices.

3. METCO parents by and large value education highly for their children, and it may be that in the suburbs they unite with parents who expect excellence from their schools to a degree not found in the city. Again this is a debatable and highly tentative statement, but it may point to an operating principle. Expectations for performance are among the important determinants of results; this is true in the case of an individual teacher's expectations of students, and it also may operate in the expectations which a group of people in a "client system" have for any given institution. Health officials have sometimes said that where people expect good service, efficiency, courtesy, and promptness, that expectation helps the system to produce better results. Where the group expectations are lessened over the course of time, the actual performance may be reduced in effectiveness. The untested assumption here is that the percentage of suburban people who both value education highly and have the time to put into making the educational system responsive to them may be greater than in the city. Thus highly motivated minority parents, by involving their children in METCO, are moving them into a system which expects and in which the client group expects success. By placing their children in a suburban school system, METCO parents place them in a system in which there are higher expectations of excellence. Those expectations affect the performance of students.

THE SUBURBAN RESPONSE TO METCO

As a white person, a suburbanite, and one who has frequently moved among teachers and citizens in a large number of communities which are host towns for METCO, it is easier to speak with assurance about the suburban response than it is to say why black families value METCO. The following is an attempt to categorize a variety of suburban responses to METCO; some of these are specific responses to METCO, and some simply state a part of the general suburban environment in which METCO operates.

1. There is in each receiving suburban community a group of people highly dedicated to the presence of, the success of, and the expansion of METCO. Often this is a small group, including both parents

and concerned citizens who are not parents; there is usually within this group a core of people who give continuity to community leadership in support of METCO over the years. These are the same people one meets in every struggle for suburban participation in the civil rights and human rights movements. Their interests in supporting METCO can probably be summarized under three concerns: (a) the provision of quality education for minority urban students, (b) the value of interracial contacts for children in white towns, largely deprived of knowing people of other races, and (c) the value of METCO as a desegregation mechanism, hoping that through the presence of METCO a given community might be moved to increase minority hiring in school and other town positions, and that in other small ways the intransigent patterns of white suburban ghettos might be changed.

2. There are those in the suburban communities who express pleasure that the suburbs can "help" the children and families of "the city." Here the motivation for support of METCO is largely paternalistic and involves clear assumptions of suburban superiority, and usually of white superiority. Among this group the expected response from METCO is one of gratitude, and any criticism of the suburb is likely to be received as ungratefulness. Support for METCO among this group is easily eroded.

3. In most suburban receiving communities there are people whose lack of enthusiasm for METCO is couched in terms of fear of metropolitan schemes in general, complaints about the "cost" of METCO, concerns that it would be better for the state to pour comparable monies into the improvement of Boston schools, and a variety of other stated arguments against the presence of METCO.

4. There are in many suburban communities, both where METCO is present and where it is not, groups who express open hostility to METCO. These people will appear at town meetings to vote against METCO being invited into the town and they will oppose expansion of METCO. In some cases it is clear that this resistance is directly related to groups whose existence is an offshoot from organized resistance to desegregation orders in Boston. The hostility frequently becomes blatantly racist, and clippings from local community newspapers record openly racist comments in arguments at town meetings, school committee meetings, and sometimes in the schools themselves.

5. *Within the school systems receiving METCO students there is a wide range of response to METCO.* In some cases administrative and teaching staff are supportive and move quickly to provide the necessary support services which will provide a good learning environment and respond to the special needs of the METCO students. In other cases there is a general inertia, a failure to see problems or to regard them as important. In rare cases there is open and obvious resistance to changes within the system which must be made if METCO is to be successful in a particular community. This range of response is present not only between receiving communities but within each community.

FUNDING PROBLEMS

METCO faces a continual task of maintaining its funding. The growth pattern described previously is very much dependent upon funding which comes from the state legislature. If the state experiences a "lean" year financially or if the political winds are against METCO, funding will not be increased. In these years of inflation, that has amounted in some cases to a cut, necessitating a reduction in METCO staff and services. Such action prevents any expansion of METCO, even though suburban communities may be ready to receive more students.

Yearly budget debates demand great time and energy on the part of METCO staff, and budgetary concerns occupy a priority which might better be given to educational matters. A method should be found to assure a more secure funding base at the state level; some superintendents have suggested a three-year funding plan, which would clearly allow for more sound, long-range educational planning. It is highly unlikely that such a plan would be acceptable to the legislature when the rest of the state budget is debated on an annual basis.

The determination of local costs is also a problem. The state reimburses local school districts for the cost of providing education to METCO students. A formula has been devised as a standard for per-pupil reimbursement. However, this formula probably provides more than the actual cost of educating METCO students in many cases, and therefore some receiving towns may be actually making a profit from the METCO program. There is need for accountability which will ensure fair and just budget levels for METCO in all cases.

CONDITIONS WHICH MAKE METCO EFFECTIVE

Evaluating the effectiveness of METCO over the twelve years of its existence and in a number of situations, it is clear that there are particular conditions which contribute to its success. Where any combination of these conditions is absent the program is significantly weakened. The following suggestions are not in any prioritized order, nor do they encompass all the ingredients of success, but these will outline some factors which are positive contributors to METCO's effectiveness.

1. *The provision of adequate support services.* It is absolutely essential that there be a strong, highly committed, skilled METCO coordinator in each receiving town. Clear lines of responsibility to METCO must be established, as well as to the local school system. Assistance to the METCO staff and coordinators must come in the form of bus monitors, tutors, guidance services, and educational specialists who must be readily available and trained to respond to the needs of individual minority students.

2. *The employment of minority school staff.* Black and other minority students in the METCO program are bused from Boston into suburbs which are usually well over 95 percent white in population, and into school systems which reflect that homogeneity. It is of great importance that black children both see and have an opportunity to relate to school staff of their own race. In a time when teaching positions are at a premium, this means that there must be a strong, consciously directed effort on the part of school systems to recruit and place minority teachers, counselors, administrators, and specialists. Other staff placements such as secretarial positions or food services can also employ minority persons and thus provide an organizational climate which is multiracial.

3. *The expansion of teacher training.* If the educational system commits itself to an *educational task* of preparing students to live in a multiracial, multicultural society, then it must involve its teaching staff in training which will provide them with insights and skills necessary for the development of multicultural education. Administrators, teachers, and others who have direct contact with METCO students should be involved in the expansion of professional skills which will include an understanding of multicultural education con-

cepts, curriculum development skills, and ways to foster positive student attitudes towards racial, ethnic, and cultural differences.

4. *There must be a conscious, long-range effort toward the development of multicultural curriculum and multicultural resources.* This is related to teacher training but includes in addition the need for a system-wide and system-supported effort in curriculum development. Individual teachers can contribute to this effort through the development of specific units of study, but if a school system is to become one which adopts the educational task of preparation for living in a pluralistic society, there are implications for curriculum development which must be implemented on a system-wide basis.

5. *There must be a movement from desegregation toward integration.* This involves at least two considerations: In the first place it means a receiving school system must move intentionally toward the inclusion of a significant number of METCO students. For instance, keeping enrollment to seventeen METCO students in an entire school system over the course of several years without expansion is mere desegregation but not integration. It might be better to concentrate METCO students in fewer school systems, limiting them to those systems which demonstrate an intention to involve a significant number of minority students. *Secondly,* it is important that METCO students be placed whenever possible so that there are at least four to a classroom. The receiving system may "sprinkle" the METCO students more widely and in doing so meet a desegregation need of the local system; but if there is an interest in moving beyond desegregation it will be important to concentrate the few METCO students so that both minority and majority students can experience something more like integration.

6. *The creation of an institutional climate so that there may be a positive entry of METCO students into suburban schools at an early age, with follow-through to graduation from high school.* The desired end here is continuity for the child's educational experience. Two conditions are essential for early entry into the suburban schools: (1) there must be continual support for the student's growth in black identity, and (2) the receiving school system must avoid the labeling and tracking of children in the early years.

While there is substantial data from studies in numerous places to indicate that beginning the interracial school experience in the first five grades results in higher achievement for black children, in the METCO experience there is evidence that beginning a child in the early years often means that the child gets "labeled" or "tracked" at an early age. This labeling becomes cumulative, following the child through his/her academic years as an increasing burden. (Labels include such phrases as "culturally deprived" and "slow learner.") *If the receiving school system and teachers continue to label and track black youngsters, and if they do not provide adequate support for the child's growth in identity as a black person, the principle announced here should give way to a practice of assigning places simply as space is available.* The latter is, in fact, the way METCO presently makes assignments. The principle of including black children in the early grades is advisable only if the conditions indicated here are integral to the receiving school system.

For white children there is much data to indicate that the most positive attitudes toward minority children are found among those who began in integrated settings at an early age. Putting people together for their first interracial encounters at the high school level is especially difficult, since that sometimes ignites deeply imbedded irrational fears about interracial sex and marriage which are highly explosive, especially among many white people.

While racial segregation and isolation in the early, formative years become cumulative processes, so do the patterns of racism implicit in the labeling of black children. Only when a school can provide education free of these racist practices is it ready to receive METCO children at early ages as a matter of educational principle.

7. *The development of strong relationships between METCO parents and host families.* The educational component of this emphasis is the involvement of parents in the education of their children. The desegregation component is in the accomplishment of one of METCO's stated purposes, namely, "closer understanding and cooperation between urban and suburban parents and other citizens." There are numerous ways in which the host family in the receiving communities can be supportive and helpful both to the METCO students and to their parents. The host parent is "on the scene," in the town where the METCO child is enrolled, and can provide a sense for that METCO child that there is a particular home in this "strange land" where he or she is cared for in a specific way. Extra-

school-related contacts between host families and METCO families bring invaluable learnings for the white families who often have no other contact with blacks.

VALUE OF METCO AS A DESEGREGATION OPTION

The minority population of Boston involved in the METCO program are mostly black Americans. To anyone familiar with the history of this country it is no surprise that a program such as METCO is one in which once again black people pay the price for American racism. METCO is one response to a poor and segregated school system in Boston, in which it is clearly demonstrable that minority people had over the course of years received unequal treatment. That fact has been established in the 1974 findings of the court. METCO preceded the court orders by eight years and was a response to the frustration of many people who had tried for years to remedy both the poor quality and the segregated nature of the school system. In the METCO program it is black children who are bused daily, in some cases many miles into what are or what are perceived as hostile communities. It is black families whose day begins earlier throughout the school year so that children can meet bus schedules. It is black children who stand on street corners, sometimes in freezing weather, waiting for the buses, and whose days are extended by the return bus rides. It is black parents who are asked to attend parent meetings sometimes in several schools scattered miles away from home. It is black parents who find it necessary to organize across school systems to insure their children the support services they need. It is black children who are denied the daily in-school contact with peers in their own community, and who in some cases suffer criticism from them. It is black families who watch their children go into mostly white systems where they often encounter racial and cultural misunderstanding, and where black people have to educate white people about those differences. It is black children who have to encounter sometimes overt, blatant racism, and who have to be constantly on the defensive to protect their rights. While the financial cost of METCO is borne by all taxpayers, the costs in time, energy, and emotion are mostly borne by black people. The comparable costs for white people involved in the program are minimal.

Black people in Boston have clearly said that METCO is an option they value. METCO could have expanded far beyond the three thousand presently enrolled, with over twice that many children now on a waiting list. These numbers are clear evidence that in spite of the cost outlined above, black people in large numbers have chosen METCO as their option. In all of the criticism of METCO and its weaknesses, most of those who talk about cutting back or eliminating METCO are white people; that cry is seldom heard from the black community. Enrollment figures speak loudly for themselves and for many black people in Boston.

The positive factors in the METCO experience far outweigh the negatives. There are other options available to parents in Boston, but against the background of desegregation in the city schools, METCO is a clear and positive choice. As a tool for desegregation it has proven effective. It can move beyond desegregation toward integration. It has been a new opportunity for quality education for many students, and that quality of education can be improved in the ways suggested previously.

METCO has already proved itself an important, almost unique venture in quality integrated education. The ways to move it toward becoming an even stronger instance of both quality and integrated education are clearly marked out for the future.

15
Learning Together: A Report on the Regional Cultural Resources Program

School District of Philadelphia

WHAT COULD BE done to extend the children's boundaries beyond the conventional four-walled classroom to provide first-rate educational experiences at a highly motivated level with reasonable cost to the taxpayer? Every educator—from classroom teacher to school district administrator—wrestles continually with this problem. School districts across the nation constantly attempt solutions to this educational dilemma.

One solution, initiated by Mrs. Irwin Homer Breslow, then Acting Chairman of the Committee on Human Relations for the City of Philadelphia, was submitted in January, 1967, to Dr. I. Ezra Staples, who was then Associate Superintendent for Curriculum, School District of Philadelphia. In this newly conceived approach, schools were to be paired from different neighborhoods (i.e., racially, religiously, economically and socially) and relocated one morning each week over an eight-week period to study an academic subject of mutual interest.

Initial contact was made with Dr. I. M. Levitt, of the Franklin Institute, to consider a science program geared to the intermediate grades with the approval of Dr. Mark R. Shedd, Superintendent of Schools. Dr. Levitt readily accepted the idea. It was agreed that the Franklin Institute would charge approximately $1.40 for each pupil. The cost of the total program amounted to $8,000, to be divided equally between the Institute and The School District of Philadelphia. Dr. Samuel S. Lepow, Director of Science Education, set up the First Cycle, which began October, 1967. Shortly thereafter, the School

162

Board officially adopted the resolution to fund half the program and provide transportation.

Five pairs of schools comprised the First Cycle. Beginning October 30, 1967 through the following eight weeks, children from these schools arrived at the Franklin Institute at 9:30 A.M. by bus for a lecture in the Planetarium and laboratory work in a designated room, where the children, paired from different schools, worked on projects based on the Planetarium lecture. Horizontal sundials, construction and use of a telescope, and portable star projector, and the construction of a scale model earth-moon system were typical projects. At the end of each laboratory session, students were permitted to take the projects home for completion and personal use.

Goals for the Regional Cultural Resources Program were these: closer cooperation among parochial, public, and suburban schools; maximum use of Philadelphia's cultural, civic, and commercial institutions ". . . to their fullest educational capacities during underutilized hours"; and timely information from men and women creating innovations to replace outdated textbooks and the conventional classroom. The primary concern of the program is education. Mrs. Breslow continually stressed the need for first-rate, firsthand educational experiences as the major aspect of the program.

In November, 1968, Mrs. Breslow requested a meeting with Dr. Shedd and Dr. Staples to organize the remainder of the program in detail. She was concerned mainly with avoiding duplication of efforts and conflicts in objectives; pressing for meetings with the public-parochial, urban, and suburban committees; making plans for future funding of the Regional Cultural Resources Program; and involving other Philadelphia cultural facilities in similar educational contributions.

The Franklin Institute's Paired Schools Program was renamed *Outside-of-school Sequenced Science Experiences,* and the Second Cycle was scheduled to begin on January 15, 1968, for five additional pairs of schools. This was the first inclusion of schools from the Archdiocese of Philadelphia.

Reports of teachers' observations in the First Cycle were submitted to Dr. Levitt and Dr. Staples. For the most part, each stated high praise for the program. For example:

Not only were the children and teachers enthusiastic about the program, but the comments from the parents gave us the feeling that this project was the best program in science that had ever been offered.

It stimulated the children to read books on the topics presented, and the number of books borrowed from the library increased during this period.

Mrs. Marian Rinnander, teacher, Dunlap School, added:

> It is my privilege to convey to you and the members of your staff on behalf of the Dunlap children, the faculty, and the community, our appreciation for the wonderful opportunity which we have experienced by being members of your eight-week course at the Planetarium. . . . We found the course informative, interesting, and very well presented. The rapport with the children was excellent, and all of our relationships with the staff were most cordial. The projects which the children did helped to heighten the interest and gave them a feeling of participating. The experience of working with real scientists in their laboratory was invaluable. A number of the children expressed an interest in choosing a vocation as an astronomer or scientist.

Funds for the Second Cycle were provided under Title I of the United States Elementary and Secondary School Act, 1965. A total of $16,000 was granted:

Instructional Services	$8,970.00
Supplies	$2,630.00
Transportation	$4,400.00

Mrs. Breslow planned extension of the Regional Cultural Resources Program to other agencies, concentrating specifically on the Philadelphia Museum of Art and the Bell Telephone Company of Pennsylvania. At a dinner attended by Dr. Lepow, Dr. Levitt, and Dr. Staples, Mrs. Breslow said:

> . . . the idea behind the Regional Cultural Resources Program for education seems to me the most natural expression of total commitment one can find. No longer can each segment in our community say, 'Let John do it,' or 'That's his department.' We desperately need each other's know-how, each other's help, if you will—empathy—which, parenthetically, will become History's sympathy if we do not all pull together for the good of all . . .

She also thanked Dr. Levitt for being "a community-oriented citizen" and pointed out that the Franklin Institute Science Program helped "to prove that the community can team together to make it happen."

An April 1, 1968, Mr. Alan Solomon, of the Research and Development Division for The School District of Philadelphia, forwarded the initial statistics compiled from the First Cycle at the Franklin Institute to Mrs. Breslow and Dr. Staples. The academic success of the program was evident from these statistics. Several of the observing teachers, however, thought the lessons in the Planetarium were somewhat above the children's level and hoped for a tighter link between the lecture series and the laboratory sessions in future cycles. All criticisms and suggestions were carefully noted by Mrs. Breslow and Dr. Staples for correction, addition, or deletion in subsequent cycles. It was also proposed that schools be matched in abilities to facilitate the learning process and that laboratory work stress group rather than individual projects in an effort to increase interaction between the paired schools.

Further support for the program was gained when Mrs. Breslow contacted Miss Celia Pincus, Representative of the Philadelphia Federation of Teachers; Miss Wilma Stringfellow, Director, YWCA of Philadelphia; and Mr. James H. Williams, Public Relations Manager, Bell Telephone Company of Pennsylvania. All replied promptly in a gracious and enthusiastic manner. Miss Pincus noted:

> The city of Philadelphia offers aspects of cultural, historical, commercial and industrial experiences unsurpassed anywhere. To make these resources of opportunities a real laboratory for our children is exciting, imaginative, and extremely worth while. Added to that, this program also provides a greater opportunity of meeting and working, even if only for a limited time, with children of different economic, racial and social backgrounds. . . . I strongly recommend this Program and hope that it will receive the funding and the ultimate success that it deserves.

Fortified by letters of support from diversified segments of the community, Dr. Shedd submitted a second and somewhat larger request for federal funds under Title I of the United States Elementary and Secondary School Act of 1965, for the amount of $25,000 to be allotted as follows:

Instructional Services	$16,000.00
Supplies	$ 3,000.00
Transportation	$ 6,000.00

During the early summer of 1968, Dr. Staples and Mrs. Breslow met Miss Jane Taylor, Educational Director for the Bell Telephone

Company, to seek Bell's participation in the Regional Cultural Resources Program. As anticipated, Miss Taylor was eager to formulate plans and discuss materials to be covered in classes at the Bell Telephone Building.

At the conclusion of the Second Cycle ten students from the Elkin School were interviewed in regard to the amount of interaction with parochial school children at the Franklin Institute and after regular school hours. It was discovered that many of the Elkin children had friends attending parochial school; but since the St. Ludwig School is located quite a distance from Elkin, very little carryover in friendships was noted. Mr. Solomon concluded: "Interaction must be attributed to the environment rather than the program."

The most frequently stated comment on the teachers' evaluation sheets was that on days scheduled for the Planetarium series, no students were absent. All schools agreed that attendance increased on days scheduled for meetings at the Franklin Institute, attesting to the genuine interest of students involved in the Paired Schools Project.

At this time Mrs. Breslow took this opportunity to point out to Mr. Paul D'Ortona, President of City Council, that the integration of races, religions, socioeconomic groups had been accomplished very quietly in the Regional Cultural Resources Program and that this type of program featuring educational excellence and *fostering integration as a bonus by-product* was labeled a success.

Teacher evaluation questionnaires on the Second Cycle indicated general agreement that the children were interested in this learning experience and that each lecture was well planned and delivered. The teachers wanted a continuation of the program. Adverse comments were that lectures were sometimes isolated from projects constructed in the following lab sessions, that certain classes were not able to grasp abstract concepts as well as others, and that it might be more efficacious to match the academic achievement levels of the paired schools at the initial selection.

Constructive criticism and suggestions were directed to Mrs. Breslow and Dr. Staples. Miss Rita Caputo, teacher at the Webster School, remarked: "There was too much material presented and given so rapidly that the children did not always keep up with the instructor." However, the statistics published on July 22, 1968, by Mr. Solomon contradicted her statement, since the figures demonstrated that the children made significant educational gains.

Toward the close of September a meeting was held among the program directors and representatives from the Bell Telephone Company of Pennsylvania to make final plans for the Bell contribution to the Regional Cultural Resources Program. Mrs. Ruth DeCou, School Relations Representative, and Miss Jane Taylor cooperated in this phase. All expenses (except transportation covered by The School District of Philadelphia) were paid by the Bell Telephone Company.

An eight-day program was instituted. An outline is listed below.

DAY ONE: Get acquainted: pair students from the visiting schools. Each child will wear a large, visible name tag. Brief explanation on the basic nature of business. Draw on knowledge already known by the students (class participation); include finance, production and marketing.

DAY TWO: Start lecture with "remember the student's name" activity, the winner to introduce the guest speaker from the U.S. Treasury. The importance of money in our economy.

DAY THREE: Students to set up a mock telephone company and run through some basic manipulations, including a strike and a bargaining session. Bring in facts about the stock market. Issue financial page of the daily papers and review basic stock reports.

DAY FOUR: Discuss telephone marketing in relation to the company's product; the function of advertising. Develop posters and slogans from the students.

DAY FIVE: View Western Electric film; tour the plant in operation. Discuss the problem in setting up the plant for factory productivity; discuss quality control of a product.

DAY SIX: Discuss salesmanship in relation to selling the public on the finished product. Involve billing and complaint procedures. Set up a mock business office with the students carrying out the individual roles of the company.

DAY SEVEN: A follow-up lesson in the actual plant. Students tour garage facilities and auto maintenance department. Visit the storage area of the installation.

DAY EIGHT: Discuss transportation, telephone installation, and the service field in general. Divide classes into small groups (six children); talk with lineman and installation supervisor. Visit the switchboard operations room. Listen to actual telephone messages in progress. Sum up the relationship of the telephone industry to the general public and the community.

At a dinner on October 21, 1968, plans were completed for a seven-week cycle at the sixth grade level through the Franklin Institute Program. Five pairs of schools would participate.

The general headings of the weekly lessons were the following:

1. Measurement, Reaction of Mass and Distance
2. Motion and Energy
3. Air and the Atmosphere
4. Water and Buoyancy
5. Heat
6. Light and Color
7. Electricity

At the same time, Mrs. Breslow gave Mr. Paul Grimes, Educational Staff Writer, EVENING BULLETIN, an in-depth report on the Regional Cultural Resources Program, making reference to its continued success. She stated that complimentary letters were received praising the purpose and scope of the program. Several days later, THE BULLETIN, over Mr. Grimes' by-line, published the headline: "*BOARD QUIETLY BUSES MORE PUPILS FROM PAIRED SCHOOLS TO 3RD SITE.*" The article stressed the facts presented by Mrs. Breslow in her letter to Mr. Grimes. Dr. Lepow mentioned that in the future the schools were to be paired in a geographically closer manner. Some suburban school districts were asked to participate, but none made a financial commitment.

A complaint of "tokenism" was brought to Mrs. Breslow's attention. She responded strongly that the only evidence of "tokenism" was the small scale of the program itself and that the Regional Cultural Resources Program ". . . could handle as many children as the monies allotted to it." She expressed her firm commitment to the program, citing its success and expressing her fervent hope to expand its scope.

The formulation of the Social Studies–History Program at the Philadelphia Museum of Art was devised for the fifth grade level to include areas, objects, facilities, and resource materials found in the Museum itself. The schools were to be paired in a manner similar to the Franklin Institute phase of the project. The program was organized for a seven-week period:

1. How People Lived in America (1750–1850 country life)
2. How People Lived in America (1750–1850 city life)
3. Tour of the Maritime Museum (stress trade)
4. Pennsylvania Dutch Way of Life
5. Crafts of the Period, Furniture, Pottery, etc.
6. Rural Crafts, Country Furniture, Tools, Pottery, etc.
7. Culminating Activity, Display of Projects, Art Work, etc.

Later, Dr. Staples notified Mrs. Breslow that Mr. Paul Long and his staff were making progress in regard to the coming program. Also, point seven from the above list changed to include the role of Afro-Americans and their contributions to the culture of the twentieth century.

Another cycle at the Franklin Institute commenced January 20, 1969 on the sixth-grade level in the area of general science under the title Out-of-school Sequenced Science Experiences for a seven-week plan. Again five pairs of schools participated. Topics areas were identical to the previous cycle.

Miriam Sue Brandt, teacher at the Adaire School, submitted the following comments:

The projects helped instill interest in the lectures. The instructors coped with the discipline problem quickly and gained rapport with the students in a short time.

In a letter from the Wright School, Miss S. LeWinter interjected:

Teachers should be given similar courses during their teacher-training years, but the vocabulary was a bit above the average fifth-grade child.

A significant survey on Cycle One was published concerning the choices of the paired-school pupils at the conclusion of that initial eight-week course.

Not one of the eighty-six children from the Finletter, Carnell, and Henry schools chose another student from the paired schools. This

Paired Schools	No. of Students Responding	No. of Out-Group Choices
Henry	25	0
Dunlap	22	10
Carnell	27	0
Meade	26	8
Forrest	27	4
Ludlow	22	12
Kenderton	29	9
Greenberg	36	8
Finletter	34	0
F. Read	33	2

is a profound statistic. To the casual observer it may appear that the program is a failure in this area; on the other hand, it clearly indicates the drastic need for additional pupil contact. Communication between youngsters is vital. More similar projects should reach children, so that they may interact while involved in an academic effort.

Before concluding this report, we would like to point out very clearly the relative low cost of these programs. The low financial expenditures for this program during an inflationary period should be a significant factor when considering the worth of the Regional Cultural Resources Program.

The following letter published in THE EVENING BULLETIN, November 4, 1968, promulgated most emphatically the intrinsic worth of the Regional Cultural Resources Program:

> I have read with interest the article in THE BULLETIN about the science programs at the Franklin Institute which involve paired schools. We are also involved in an interschool program, bringing together youngsters of different backgrounds for varied learning experiences.
>
> It seems that an essential element in these projects must be the opportunity for talking about the activity or something else of mutual interest as often as possible and over a long period of time—more than six or eight weeks.
>
> However, the success of such programs cannot really be measured in terms of how many "friendships" develop. Perhaps one day, in a tense situation, a child will remember that such contacts were possible and, in fact, comfortable. Perhaps some children will begin to

think of individuals, not groups, because of these classes. Perhaps parents will learn that the critical issue is that what has happened is exciting and valuable to their children as they share what they have learned with other children.

The full impact of such experiences will be measured if we do not have repetitions of the events of the last few weeks in Philadelphia, ten years from now. To insure this, one hopes for an expansion of good interschool programs.

(Signed)

Mrs. Raymond Berkowitz

16
School Integration:
The Witness of the Church

Ruth C. Wick

THE DOCTRINE THAT all men are created equal is a major premise of the Declaration of Independence. The founding fathers consistently insisted that this proposition was the keystone on which our nation was to be built. How that equality was expressed and promoted was, however, another question, and our continued failure over two hundred years to implement this ideal lies heavy on the American conscience. Perhaps our failure has been because we have understood or interpreted this declaration "that all men are created equal" erroneously. The statement is unambiguously clear, but too often we have acted as if this equality is something to be earned, a goal to be achieved by some special efforts which "give" this equality to us on merit. We do not work to be "equal" or to have equality. We begin with the fact that to be equal is "self-evident."

A peculiar role of the Christian and the church, and indeed of the community of the Jewish faith also, is to always press this point. Equality is the beginning, not the result or end goal. Christians and Jews must both maintain the proclamation of the ontological assumption as theological truth, namely: equality is granted to all because all are persons created by one God. Equality is granted by God, the Creator, and no empirical differences can erase this reality. The First Article of the Creeds is a confession of that equality:

I believe in God, the Father Almighty, creator of heaven and earth.

(Apostles' Creed)

or

We believe in one God, the Father, the Almighty, maker of heaven and earth, of all that is, seen and unseen.

(Nicene Creed)

Because we believe and confess this, we believe also that our equality as persons is an equality of worth before God and is established by our very creation.

We also affirm that God who created is the living God of history. This is a reminder of our past and our failures, and also of the possibilities for the future. To affirm equality must involve all Christians in making it real in practice—that is, making real the access which all must have to participate in all dimensions of life within the civil order, to eliminate the gap between professed equality and the actual and unjust discriminations which deny that equality.

Creation establishes our equality; life in faith in our Lord Jesus Christ is the assurance of the unity of all persons. Equality and unity belong together. Through Baptism all Christians are inextricably related to all persons and to all creation and are called to live in unity and in reconciliation with all persons and with all creation. It would be presumptuous to claim that the actual internal structures of the church and indeed of our common life as Christians present anything but a distorted image of this relationship of equality and unity. Yet we are called to live and witness in word and deed to this equality and to this unity, as liberated and reconciled persons.

To be equal (equality), as we understand it, is a free gift of worth before God and therefore before all persons. To affirm this equality is to make it real in practice. Persons differ in endowments and circumstances, but all are equally entitled to the things and protections they need to live in a meaningful relationship to other persons in community. In the educational area this means equal access to the educational opportunities in a community. Where such equal access is not present for some persons, then others are living a life of special privilege. This privilege, bought at the expense of equal access and opportunity for all, denies the freedom of the individual and is tyranny.

The National Council of the Churches of Christ in the United States of America in its 1962 statement *The Churches and the Public Schools* stated:

As Christians we believe that every individual has a right to an education aimed at the full development of his (her) capacities as a human being created by God, his (her) character as well as intellect. We are impelled by love of neighbor to seek maximum educational opportunities in order that he (she) may prepare for responsible participation in the common life.

When there is a gap between our professed understanding of equality and the provision of equal access and equal opportunity to the educational possibilities in a community, then there is unjust discrimination which denies to some persons their freedom to live fully as responsible, participating individuals in the society in which they may be placed. This is a violation of the person and of personal freedom. This right of equal opportunity and the right to be accepted as equal is what justice requires in response to the human need for freedom itself.

THE ROLE THE CHURCH MAY TAKE

The church lives in and for the world, but not of the world. It has the responsibility to break out from any established cultural/ social milieu and to support all efforts for racial justice, equal access to opportunities within the society without regard to race or creed, and all efforts in the community to bring about understanding at points of racial tension. The church does this by being informed of the needs and the options in any particular community and by directing its efforts to specific times, places, and circumstances where there are expressions of racial discrimination or evidences of injustice. In the total society it works for the removal of all laws which restrict, discriminate, or unjustly characterize any person because of race, color, or creed. Further, the church has the responsibility to encourage individual members in their understanding both of the situation which is being addressed and the biblical imperatives for justice, equality, and freedom. It has the further responsibility for informing its members of the social statements of the church as they apply to these issues, and to encourage and support its members as they work for necessary change in society.

The church and its members should be involved in the community in which they live and should give leadership to all efforts for peaceful change for justice and equal access to the educational systems, and support and give leadership to all efforts for developing "quality education" for all persons in the community. Such leadership is important. John Buggs, Staff Director of the U.S. Commission on Civil Rights, stressed this when he stated,

> The single most important ingredient in achieving peaceful and successful desegregation is affirmative leadership by those entrusted with that community's social, economic, educational, political, and religious institutions.[1]

The church also has the responsibility of encouraging its members to take seriously their responsibility for the quality of the education offered in their school system and to work actively as citizens for the improvement of public education. This may mean for some members greater involvement in the support of the schools in which their children study; for others, accepting responsibility in the political process and the community governance of the educational system; for those who teach and administer, support of all efforts to provide quality education with open access for all. It means understanding and accepting change when this is necessary and desirable. The church and its members cannot escape their responsibility in the area of desegregation and integration of the public educational system in their community for the good of the entire society. Finally, the church must take responsibility for the schools supported by the church so that discrimination on the basis of race, color, or creed is eliminated wherever it may be found. To do less is "institutional disobedience" to the intent and will of the Lord of the church.

The 1978 Lutheran Church in America Social Statement *Human Rights: Doing Justice in God's World* sets for us a rationale for the church's involvement in an area such as school integration when it states:

> God calls the church in every time and place to proclaim righteousness, to struggle against injustice, and to care for the creation. It is therefore fitting that we in the Lutheran Church in America, as one embodiment of God's people in the world, declare our understanding of human rights and take our stand with all who work and suffer to advance freedom, equality, and justice in ways that more truly reflect God's intention for humanity.[2]

This statement also affirms:

> God has redeemed us by the Cross and Resurrection of Jesus the Christ, has incorporated us into Christ's Body, the church, and has called us to loving service in the world. God calls us to serve, both

corporately and individually, in the ongoing struggle for justice and human rights.[3]

Also the statement reminds us that

corporately as the church, and individually as Christians, we participate in this struggle not out of a love of power but by the power of the divine love for the whole world. In Christ we have been freed from a preoccupation with our own rights in order to give ourselves to the securing of justice for our neighbors in the worldwide human family.[4]

DESEGREGATION AND INTEGRATION, ISSUES OF JUSTICE

The corporate church as well as individual Christians must address desegregation and integration as issues of justice. This is a task for the entire Christian community, and indeed for all communities of faith. Few issues in our time have generated so much controversy as the matter of justice in the area of education: the acknowledgment that every child, regardless of race, color, or creed, has a right to equal access to the educational opportunities in a community. There should be no doubts, no procrastination or rationalization, no need for court orders to guarantee this simple right, this justice for all persons in our society. Biblical theology would say that justice cannot be denied, because it is rooted in God, the One who is just.

The Judeo-Christian heritage reminds all of us of God's demands on his people for justice. In the Book of Micah we read,

> He has showed you, O man, what is good,
> and what does the Lord require of you
> but to do justice, and to love kindness,
> and to walk humbly with your God?
> (Micah 6:8)

The Hebrew Bible speaks of the people of God united to God by a bond of his making—his covenant. In return those people pledged themselves to an exclusive loyalty to the Lord, a loyalty which could only be adequately realized in a society whose life reflected the known moral demands of this holy God. These are a people to be used by God in the fulfillment of his gracious purpose for all mankind—where all of his people are called to do justly, to reflect in their attitude toward one another God's attitude to them. The prophet Amos reminded the people that the God whose very nature is steadfast love demands from his people that they "hate evil, and love good, and establish justice in the gate" (Amos 5:15).

Amos calls the people to root out from the life of the society conditions under which persons "sell the righteous [i.e., innocent] for silver, and the needy for a pair of shoes, that trample the head of the poor into the dust of the earth, and turn aside the way of the afflicted" (Amos 2:7). To protect the unprotected is to do justice. Isaiah bids the people, "cease to do evil, learn to do good; seek justice, correct oppression" (Isa. 1:16–17).

The struggle for justice is a constant struggle. This country has been shaped from the earliest time by the anguish of the immigrant; of the American black for whom this country was from the beginning a land of bondage; of the American Indian relegated to reservations, shattered as persons and as tribes; of more recent arrivals from Puerto Rico, Mexico, Vietnam, Latin and South America who suffer incredible language difficulties with resulting prejudice and discrimination even in the educational systems. The deprivations of these and other "minorities" constitute a dominant pattern in the fabric of American life. In spite of all of the promises of the Constitution and Supreme Court decisions, we still find that our life together is filled with injustices and is too often marred by racial discrimination and intergroup conflict.

We must be concerned about communities where the educational processes are disrupted by strife, conflict, tensions, deep-rooted emotions, and often severe violence. Some of this has been aimed at denying equal access to educational opportunities. Because of endemic obsessions about race, the black minority has occupied a place in the American spectrum by which the relative freedom from discrimination of all other minorities may be measured.

We have come a long distance from the concept of "separate but equal" (*Plessy v. Ferguson*, 1896) to the concept that "separate is not equal" (*Brown*, 1954). Today, we know that persons isolated and segregated by intention and design on racial grounds are in a very real sense deprived, and that this deprivation takes place in the midst of potentially enriching educational experiences provided through our system of public education. Twenty-five years have elapsed since the Supreme Court made it clear that segregated education has a negative effect upon children, that separate school systems are not equal, and constitutional rights of children are not to be denied. Desegregation was to be accomplished "with all deliberate speed." But this has not been the case in this past quarter century, and evidence reveals a history of opposition and delays in almost every community. Despite the varied problems of public education today, the widespread development, especially in southern states, of the private "Christian academies" epitomizes as does nothing else our divisions in community and our inability to exercise justice.

Yet there are in many places persons who are working for justice in the area of education, who believe that separate is not equal and that equal access to a good education in our society today is a basic right for all persons. These persons and institutions work in the belief that our educational experiences must be so organized that they will enable and facilitate our ability to live meaningful and productive lives in the midst of the reality of our pluralism and our diversity. Enlightened educational, church, and civic leaders recognize that there are many ways to desegregate schools: school attendance lines may be redrawn, schools may be paired, larger physical facilities may be built to serve larger and more diverse enrollments, magnet schools may be established. Transportation of students is another tool to accomplish desegregation.

Others in this book have dealt with the specifics in many of the options noted above and have suggested additional possibilities. I shall not attempt to address the validity of these various approaches, but I would like to comment briefly on the problem of transportation of students for desegregation purposes, especially since in this period in our history more and more attention is being given to "local control," neighborhood schools, family involvement, and so forth. In the area of desegregation, there is little doubt that the greatest opposition has been centered around the subject of busing, or as those who oppose it say, "forced busing." Yet if we examine all of the reasons for providing transportation for students in the educational systems, we find that a very small percentage of the busing for education in the United States is for the purposes of racial desegregation. Some have estimated it to be less than 20 percent. This fact is indeed interesting, especially since so many of the opponents of busing often declare that they are for racial desegregation but against "forced busing" to accomplish this goal. The question which must then be raised is whether the resistance to busing, and indeed to other aspects of the desegregation process, does not actually reflect a deep-rooted racism, both personal and institutional, in our society.

DESEGREGATION AND SCHOOL INTEGRATION, ISSUES OF RACISM

We need indeed to admit that racism cuts deep into all lives and social structures. We need also to admit that desegregation has not always provided positive changes toward "quality education," nor has racism been eliminated. We need to recognize that racism can and does thrive in either a segregated or a desegregated educational system. The real issue, therefore, is not what means are used to desegregate a school system. The real issue for our society is primarily racism in all of its manifest forms: segregated housing, inequities in economic opportunities, restrictive covenants, redlining by banks and insurance companies, the lack of opportunities for equal access to educational opportunities. Racism is damaging not only to the one discriminated against but also to the person engaged in the discrimination. Racial segregation is a blight on all communities where it exists. Racism breeds and perpetuates prejudice and discrimination even as it is also the result of such prejudice and discrimination. It breeds inequities and injustices, nurtures destructive tensions and violence. We must be concerned therefore about the realization of racial integration in the total society, in all its structures and institutions, including the church. The expected goal of integrated quality education, accessible to all persons, will be fulfilled only as we oppose all forms of racial isolation.

The Lutheran Church in America in its 1964 Social Statement *Race Relations* states:

> The current racial revolution has thrust the church into a time of travail and perplexity, but also of opportunity and hope. Injustice which for a long time was either ignored, rationalized, or mutely borne is now seen more clearly for what it actually is. Injurious discrimination based on race is a violation of God's created order, of the meaning of redemption in Christ, and of the nature of the church. Implicit in such discrimination often are unbiblical views of God and of man. The church must oppose such false views with all the power of the truth of God; in its prayer and worship, in its theological thought, in the nurture of the personal life, in its institutional forms, and in individual and corporate action in society.[5]

In opposing all forms of racial segregation we most often use the two terms *desegregation* and *integration*. These terms are often used interchangeably, as if they had exactly the same meaning. I would suggest that while they are related, they have quite different meanings and implications. Desegregation is primarily the realignment of persons to provide a more balanced racial mix. Desegregation does not necessarily of itself reduce racial isolation.

Integration, on the other hand, implies qualitative interpersonal relationships in which persons of various ethnic, cultural, and racial origins relate to one another. Integration involves a person in mutual respect, appreciation, and cooperation with another person. Integration requires a genuine affective response to one another which can be cultivated but not mandated. Integration is, however, dependent on desegregation. It is not possible for integration to take place in an educational system which is basically segregated. Therefore desegregation is an essential component for the development of an integrated society and an integrated system of education. Desegregation, if accompanied by other programs to achieve affective experiences, can result in that quality of human relationships we would define as integration. It is the goal of integration to which we aspire: an integration which respects and enhances cultural and racial diversity, an integration which adds variety and richness to the whole of society. An integrated society is a society where persons of differing ethnic, cultural, and racial backgrounds live together in mutual appreciation of each other and in mutual cooperation, and where there is achieved a reasonable measure of justice and order for all persons and where quality education is available for all on an equal basis.

If quality education is to develop, it is clear that there must be a profound and radical transformation of the entire society, of our moral/ethical attitudes toward those of another race. Only then will a radical transformation of education take place.

For this reason we must take seriously the fact that racism is the root evil which can permeate a segregated or even a desegregated system of education. Integration is not just putting children of all races together; it is a significant and even cataclysmic change in persons, in their understanding of, appreciation for, and acceptance of persons who are different and who represent a different racial heritage and a different cultural experience. The significance of the word integration cannot be overstated, for it applies to the well-being of our society as a whole, not just to its present educational systems. Racial isolation at all levels, whether in segregated or desegregated systems, creates division in our society. Such division threatens every citizen.

In the Judeo-Christian belief, God is the Creator of all persons. In Genesis we read:

> Then God said, "Let us make man in our image, after our likeness; and let them have dominion over the fish of the sea, and over the birds of the air, and over the cattle, and over all the earth, and over every creeping thing that creeps upon the earth." So God created man in his own image, in the image of God he created him; male and female he created them. And God blessed them, and God said to them, "Be fruitful and multiply, and fill the earth and subdue it; and have dominion over the fish of the sea and over the birds of the air and over every living thing that moves upon the earth."
>
> (Gen. 1:26–29)
>
> And God saw everything that he had made, and behold, it was very good.
>
> (Gen. 1:31)

The thought of the divine image in the creation of man provides a definition of our relationship with each other which can never be lost for all who wear the human face. As creatures of one God, all peoples are members of the one great family. The list of nations in Genesis 10—unique in ancient Eastern literature—makes no claim for Israel of any fundamentally different natural capacity or "inherited" nobility which might set it apart from the rest of humanity. The Hebrew Bible knows nothing of races which are "naturally inferior" or unworthy of designation as human. Mankind appears at the beginning of Israel's records as a single entity and continues as such under God the Creator. In the New Testament this understanding is continued in the life, work, and teaching of Jesus the Christ, Son of God, Redeemer. Paul writes in his letter to the Galatians:

> Now before faith came, we were confined under the law, kept under restraint until faith should be revealed. So that the law was our custodian until Christ came, that we might be justified by faith. But now that faith has come, we are no longer under a custodian; for in Christ Jesus you are all sons of God, through faith. For as many of you as were baptized into Christ have put on Christ. There is neither Jew nor Greek, there is neither slave nor free, there is neither male nor female; for you are all one in Christ Jesus. And if you are Christ's, then you are Abraham's offspring, heirs according to promise.
>
> (Gal. 3:23–29)

God has created persons in one human family (Acts 17:26). Racial segregation in any form is a threat to every person; it denies the intent of God's creation and is disobedience to his will for all mankind to live together in community and in harmony with each other; it destroys the possibility of true life together in community; it destroys the human dignity of both the racist and the victim.

In the Social Statement of the Lutheran Church in America of 1964, *Race Relations*, the church states:

> We pray that, our unity of fellowship being manifest, we may hold out to a broken world the salvatory meaning of God's fatherhood. This requires a unity that is visible and tangible.
>
> It requires Christians to seek out and receive one another as brothers (and sisters) without regard to nation, race, or culture.
>
> It means that a racially segregated church is institutional disobedience . . .
>
> The substance of the church's action in all matters of racial discrimination is determined for it and stands as a permanent testimony each time the church prays or confesses its faith or proclaims its message.[6]

The Reverend Ricardo T. Potter, Staff Associate for Racial and Ethnic Concerns of the Division of Church and Society, National Council of the Churches of Christ in the United States of America, has stated this concern eloquently:

> Where there is no equality, there is no pride; where there is no justice, there is no dignity; and where there is no love, there is no self-esteem. And, no society, no nation can be fully healthy and happy without pride, dignity, and self-esteem.
>
> Let's then say it this way: we can put all black schools on a par with all white schools of the best quality. If this is done, some say, it will be unnecessary to worry about integration. Children of all races will then have equal educational opportunities everywhere. But, my brother, one of the most important ingredients of education is hope, hope for a better future, hope to become an accepted member of society, hope for an end to discrimination, hope for dignity and self-determination. Racially isolated schools do not provide or satisfy any of these needs. Instead they spell segregation, and no matter how benevolent segregation could be, it is rejection. Segregation is not justice; it is the classic symbol of centuries-long traditions of racism.[7]

NOTES

1. John Buggs, *Desegregation without Turmoil: The Role of the Multi-racial Community Coalition in Preparing for Smooth Transition* (New York: National Conference of Christians and Jews, 1976), p. 3.

2. *Human Rights: Doing Justice in God's World*, A Social Statement of the Lutheran Church in An erica, Adopted by the Ninth Biennial Convention, 1978, p. 1.

3. Ibid., p. 5.

4. Ibid., p. 5.

5. *Race Relations*, A Social Statement of the Lutheran Church in America, Adopted by the Second Biennial Convention, 1964, p. 1.

6. Ibid., pp. 1–2.

7. Ricardo T. Potter, "True Integration or Justice within the Educational System," *School Desegregation: Community Preparation and the Role of the Church* (study booklet), National Council of the Churches of Christ in the U.S.A., 1977, pp. 16–17.

About the Editors

MURRAY FRIEDMAN is Middle Atlantic States Director of the American Jewish Committee and teaches courses on minority problems and urban sociology at LaSalle College in Philadelphia. He has edited a collection of essays, *Overcoming Middle Class Rage*, and contributed the introduction to this volume.

ROGER MELTZER, Assistant Director of the Middle Atlantic Region of the American Jewish Committee, has a multimedia background as a journalist and has been extensively involved in civil rights activities, interfaith and intergroup relations projects and community development programs. He served as Desegregation Committee Chairman of the Philadelphia Interfaith Task Force for Quality Public Education.

CHARLES MILLER is Assistant to the President of the Lutheran Synod of Southeast Pennsylvania with primary responsibility in social services and social ministry.

About the Contributors

DERRICK A. BELL, JR., is Professor of Law at Harvard University and former counsel to the National Association for the Advancement of Colored People, handling over three hundred desegregation cases in the 1960s. He has written numerous articles on school desegregation, including "Serving Two Masters: Integration Ideals and Client Interests in School Desegregation Litigation."

HOMER C. FLOYD is Executive Director of the Pennsylvania Human Relations Commission. His agency has peacefully desegregated twenty-two school districts in the state and has obtained Commonwealth Court decisions to create racial balance in the Philadelphia and Pittsburgh school districts.

IRVING M. LEVINE is National Director of the American Jewish Committee's Institute on Pluralism and Group Identity and is a leading contributor to the development, research, and advocacy of the "new ethnicity" movement.

JAMES A. BANKS is Professor of Education at the University of Washington and has written extensively in the field of ethnic studies. His works include *Black Self-Concept: Implications for Education and Social Science* and *Multi-Ethnic Education: Practices and Promises*.

THOMAS VITULLO-MARTIN is an independent policy analyst located in New York City, specializing in education and urban development.

ROCHELLE L. STANFIELD is a staff correspondent for the *National Journal*, specializing in education, intergovernmental relations, urban affairs, housing and community development, and transportation.

WARD SINCLAIR is a staff writer at the *Washington Post*.

THOMAS SOWELL is Professor of Economics at the University of California at Los Angeles. He has written for numerous U.S., Canadian, and British journals and his publications include *Black Education: Myths and Tragedies, Race and Economics,* and *Education and Parental Responsibility.*

JAMES S. COLEMAN, formerly of Johns Hopkins University, is Professor of Sociology at the University of Chicago. A former member of the President's Science Advisory Committee, he has published widely in public and professional journals on both sociology and education and is the principal author of the U.S. Department of Health, Education, and Welfare's pioneering work *Equality of Education Opportunity* as well as chief architect of the "white flight" debate among social scientists.

THOMAS F. PETTIGREW is Professor of Social Psychology and Sociology at Harvard University and was Fellow at the Center for Advanced Study in the Behavioral Sciences at Stanford University. He and Robert L. Green are coauthors of the Harvard Educational Review's "School Desegregation in Large Cities: A Critique of the Coleman 'White Flight' Thesis."

ROBERT L. GREEN is Dean of the College of Urban Development and Professor of Educational Psychology at Michigan State University.

ROBERT L. CRAIN and RITA E. MAHARD, researchers for the Management Sciences Department of the Rand Corporation, are coauthors of "Desegregation and Black Achievement," presented to the National Review Panel on School Desegregation Research at Duke University's Institute of Policy Sciences and Public Affairs. Their comprehensive research appeared in Duke University's law journal, *Law and Contemporary Problems.*

JOHN R. VANNONI is principal of the successfully integrated "magnet" Philadelphia High School for the Creative and Performing Arts.

HORACE SELDON is an ordained minister of the United Church of Christ and Executive Director of Community Change, Inc., which works to facilitate suburban participation in Boston's METCO program of voluntary cross-district desegregation. An adjunct member of the faculty at the Andover Theological School, he is active in the Massachusetts Coalition for Human Rights and Chairman of its Urban-Suburban Education Committee.

RUTH C. WICK is Secretary for Social Concerns of the Lutheran Church in America's Department for Church and Society and Education Chairperson for the National Council of Churches.